Beyond the Pale

Dramatic Writing from
First Nations Writers & Writers of Colour

editors

Yvette Nolan
Betty Quan
George Bwanika Seremba

Playwrights Canada Press
Toronto • Canada

Playwrights Canada Press operates with the generous assistance of
The Canada Council - Writing and Publishing Section, and Theatre
Section, and the Ontario Arts Council.

Canadian Cataloguing in Publication Data
Beyond the pale : dramatic writing from First Nations writers & writers
of colour

ISBN 0-88754-542-4
1. Canadian drama (English) - 20th century.* 2. Canadian drama (English) -
Minority authors.* 3. Canadian drama (English) - Indian authors.*
4. Canadian drama (English) - Inuit authors.* 5. Canadian drama (English) -
Métis authors.* I. Nolan, Yvette. II. Quan, Betty, 1964-   . III. Seremba,
George, 1958-   .

PS8307.B48   1996   C812'.5408089   C96-930122-7
PR9196.3.B18   1996

First edition: March, 1996.
Printed and bound in Winnipeg, Manitoba, Canada.

table of contents

foreword

This is a book of different voices. The voices of playwrights that are now, happily, starting to be produced more on professional stages of all sizes.

They tell the stories of a great number of Canadians — stories of survival against almost impossible odds. These are stories that need to be told, and heard, because they tell us of the lives of the people who live around us.

These increasingly confident voices are those of the first languages ever spoken in this land, and of the many different languages spoken in other countries and now spoken here. They are also the voices of many distinct dialects of English. They are, moreover, uniquely different perspectives, that are now inarguably voices of this country.

There is great pain and sorrow here, and great joy.

Tony Hamill
Managing Editor

Coups and Calypso

M. Nourbese Philip

M. Nourbese Philip is a poet and writer who lives in the City of Toronto. She has published four books of poetry, *Thorns, Salmon Courage, She Tries Her Tongue; Her Silence Softly Breaks,* and *Looking for Livingstone: An Odyssey of Silence* - a poem in prose and poetry.

Her first novel, *Harriet's Daughter,* was published in 1988 by Heinemann (England) and the Women's Press (Canada). The book was a finalist in the 1989 Canadian Library Association Prize for Children's Literature; the Max and Greta Abel Award for Multicultural Literature, 1990, and the Toronto Book Awards, 1990.

Her manuscript collection of poetry, "She Tries Her Tongue..." was awarded the 1988 Casa de las Americas prize for poetry. In 1990 M. Nourbese Philip was made a Guggenheim Fellow in poetry, and in 1991 became a Macdowell Fellow.

Her short stories, essays, reviews and articles have appeared in magazines and journals in Canada, the U.K. and the U.S.A., and her poetry and prose have been extensively anthologised. Her most recent works, "Frontiers: Essays and Writings in Racism and Culture", and "Showing Grit: Showboating North of the 44th Parallel" were published in November, 1992 and June, 1993 respectively.

In 1994, Nourbese Philip's short story, "Stop Frame" was awarded the Lawrence Foundation Award by the U.S. journal, *Prairie Schooner,* and in 1995 she was awarded the Arts Foundation of Toronto Award in writing and publishing.

Coups and Calypso

M. Nourbese Philip

Elvira, an African Trinidadian woman and Rohan, an Indo-Trinidadian man, who have been separated for some time, meet unexpectedly in Tobago during a coup. Rohan invites Elvira to wait out the coup with him in his holiday home. As a consequence, they are forced to re-examine the many issues, including those of identity and culture, that contributed to the break up of their marriage.

Act Two, Scene One - in the living room.

ELVIRA   (*nervous*) Did you close the back door?

                         She checks it herself.

ROHAN   We're perfectly safe here. (*as she shuts the shutters in the kitchen*) Elvira! — *please* — don't close the windows — it'll make it too hot.

ELVIRA   People can look in on us.

ROHAN   Which people?

ELVIRA   You know — the ones with penises and two balls — the same ones who go around raping women. Have I made myself clear?

ROHAN   You have.

ELVIRA   (*pacing*) When is all this going to be over? I'm shut in on this damn island, where if you're not careful and run too fast, you land in the sea; shut up in this damn house; shut up in this body of mine that is only a liability at a time like this. Why the hell doesn't America invade and put an end to all this?

ROHAN   (*laughing loudly*) I never thought I would hear the day when you would even contemplate, let alone voice such a wish. You should wash your mouth out, Elvira.

ELVIRA   I don't mean it — you know that. Forget you heard me say it. It's this waiting that I find so impossible and not knowing what's happening here.

ROHAN   Waiting — sometimes that *is* the hardest thing to do. (*pause*)

'I said to my soul be still and wait without hope/ for to hope would be to hope for the wrong thing; wait without love/ For love would be love of the wrong thing; there is yet faith/ but the faith, the love and the hope are all in the waiting/ Wait without thought, for you are not ready for thought/ so the darkness shall be the light, and the stillness the dancing.'

Why don't we finish the wine.

ELVIRA   And you want me to ask 'who's that' so that you can tell me that we doctors are badly educated.

ROHAN   But you are — focused entirely on the body with no attention given to the soul — I suppose because you can't dissect it.

She clears the table.

ELVIRA   Who was it that said there was no exam for the soul?

ROHAN
It doesn't mean that I don't believe the soul should not be nurtured. It should be mandatory for doctors and lawyers to study poetry.

He sits on the couch.

'The darkness shall be light.' How many times did I repeat that to myself? (*pause*) How many, many times, while I waited — not knowing whether you were coming: 'the darkness shall be light': would you accept my offer of marriage? 'The darkness shall be light' — two years, Elvira, two years I waited for you.

ELVIRA
I was doing my exams. (*pause*) And it was only 18 months.

ROHAN
Twenty two months to the day - waiting and going slowly mad — 'the darkness shall be light' — more mad than I knew I already was for leaving my law studies to do a degree in English literature. 'The darkness shall be light' and London was never drearier, uglier or more grim. (*pause*) The darkness *was* light eventually.

ELVIRA
Is this supposed to make me feel guilty? I do, Rohan.

ROHAN
Guilty? No. (*pause*) The mind plays such strange tricks — the only two things I remember from that time is that quotation and when the woman in the bus queue cursed me.

ELVIRA
You mean the one who put a good West Indian cussin on you? (*they laugh*)

ROHAN
The same one. I convinced myself that you had come to London and hadn't told me. The way she moved her head — so much like you. I should have known better — it was winter and we all look alike bundled up.

ELVIRA
And you went and touched the woman on her shoulder. (*he laughs*) Only it wasn't me.

ROHAN
I had no business touching her. She traced my ancestry right back to before time itself and the farther back it went the worse it became.

ELVIRA
Punctuated by a few raas cloths and bumba cloths.

ROHAN
The longer my genealogy grew, the more questionable it became. I didn't get on the bus with her — I had to wait another ten minutes. (*pause*) Seemed all I was doing in those days was waiting.

ELVIRA
You keep harping on this waiting—

ROHAN
Don't you remember anything from that time?

ELVIRA
You really want to know what I remember from those days? I remember how your family didn't want me for their great son. You forget I was here, Rohan — in Trinidad — I heard some of the stories. (*raising her voice*) You hear what happen to dat nice Rohan — Raj and Vena oldest boy, dey used to have a stall on de Main Road before — he marryin dat nigger girl from up Brown Trace. And you should see she — she black for so. She must be give him some good stoop down obeah. Is a good ting dey have other children.

ROHAN
Stop it, Elvira!

ELVIRA
(*she continues the mimicking voice*) Dis douglarisation must stop — Indian should marry Indian and African marry African, and white marry white. Dove and corbeaux should never mate although both a dem is bird. *That* is what I remember.

ROHAN
(*shouting*) I said stop it!

ELVIRA
They all blame you for killing your father — the shock of your marrying a hanoman — a monkey.

ROHAN
Enough, Elvira! Enough, I said.

He paces.

ELVIRA You started it. (*she continues washing and drying the dishes*)

ROHAN Only because being back here reminds me of you — of myself, of us — I don't know any more — maybe I want that innocence we had back then.

ELVIRA What innocence? You romanticize everything to compensate for all the pain you caused your family over me.

ROHAN That's a cruel thing to say, Elvira — a cruel thing my leaving my law studies was equally stressful for him.

ELVIRA We live in cruel times, Rohan. I didn't lose my family because of you — all Granny wanted was for me to be happy, and while Ma and Pa weren't thrilled about my marrying you, as long as I qualified and got a degree they were happy.

> *She puts down the kitchen towel and sits at the dining table.*

Your family buried you, Rohan, because you loved a Black woman — a nigger woman — and weren't content just to fuck her — behind the bushes, because everyone knows that we're loose and that's what we do — you had to go and marry her. I can't ever compensate you for that.

ROHAN I haven't ever asked you for compensation, Elvira, just your love — only your love, only your love.

ELVIRA You've always had that.

ROHAN Then why did you leave me — for fuck's sake — why?

> *She is silent.*

Talk to me — like you never would in London. I need to know why, Elvira. Come on to the porch and talk to me.

ELVIRA   Only if you call it a gallery.

ROHAN   (*laughing*) Come on to the gallery and talk with
                    me.

                        She dries her hands, turns up the radio and
                        follows him onto the porch.

***

fareWel

Ian Ross

Ian Ross was born in MacCreary, Manitoba, and spent the first five years of his life in the Metis community of Kinosta, before moving to Winnipeg, where he has resided ever since. He has spent most of his summers and holidays with family in the community of Fairford. Ian has very strong roots in rural Manitoba.

He holds a Bachelor of Arts degree from the University of Manitoba, having majored in Film, with a theatre minor. He has been writing plays for five years, and "fareWel" , at Prairie Theatre Exchange, Winnipeg, March 1996, marks his first professional production.

Ian wrote this play to share some of his experiences and observations of life on a reserve in Manitoba, as well as to explore several concerns facing native people today, such as self-government, the role of women in native politics, Bill C-31, Christian versus Traditional spirituality, and poverty. However, these concerns are not strictly limited to First Nations peoples, but to everyone in Canadian society today.

fareWel

Ian Ross

*With the failure of the welfare cheques to appear, Teddy
decides to pursue his own brand of self-government.
Using the reserve's restaurant-convenience store-coffee
shop-gas station, Teddy calls a meeting to take control
of the reserve and its future.*

> *Scene Seven. Lights come up on Walter's
> Restaurant. TEDDY has arranged some chairs,
> which await an audience. A wooden Pepsi box
> is being used as a podium. There are some
> crude signs with pictures of TEDDY on them.
> NIGGER hobbles towards the counter,
> dragging his 'crutch', and uses whatever he can
> to prop himself up.*

NIGGER   Hey, Walter. Walter. Where the hell are you? I need some med-cin. Fix my tooth for me. And my leg too. This stupid stick hurts my arm. (*throwing down the 'crutch'*) Where the hell is Walter?

> *TEDDY enters.*

TEDDY   O.K. Come sit over here. (*motioning to the chairs*)

NIGGER   I can't walk good.

TEDDY   Be a man, eh?

NIGGER   O.K. Wait.

NIGGER grabs some chips, then hobbles over to the chairs and sits down.

NIGGER   What's this anyways?

TEDDY   It's a meeting. You'll see when Melvin and them get here.

ROBERT walks in.

TEDDY   Shit.

NIGGER   What?

TEDDY   We don't need this asshole.

ROBERT   Walter? Walter? Teddy have you seen Walter?

TEDDY   Nope.

ROBERT walks behind the counter and pulls out a little book.

ROBERT   Tell Walter I came to pay my bill and left this cheque for him. (*ROBERT looks in the book and puts a cheque in it*) Nine hunerd bucks. Man. Man. Those kids'll make me go broke. Tell Walter not to let my kids charge burgers and stuff on here again unless I say it's O.K. Alright?

TEDDY   Tell him yourself.

MELVIN walks in with RACHEL and PHYLLIS.

TEDDY   Ahhh shit. Melvin I told you just to bring men.

MELVIN   I didn't bring them. They came here by themself.

TEDDY   Where's Cheezie and Rudy and those guys. I told you to bring them.

MELVIN   Cheezie's passed out and those other guys went to Little Sask for bingo.

TEDDY	For fuck sakes.
RACHEL	You're such a little shit Teddy. Just 'cause you hear I call a meeting and so you have to call one?
TEDDY	I called this meeting before you did.
RACHEL	Let's ask Walter. Walter? Walter. Where the hell's Walter?
TEDDY	He's pumping gas.
RACHEL	It doesn't matter anyways. I called this meeting first.
ROBERT	What meeting?
RACHEL	The one I set up to fix this problem with welfare.
TEDDY	That's what *this* meeting's about.
RACHEL	Good. Then we'll be talking about the same thing.
TEDDY	No. This is my meeting.
PHYLLIS	This is our meeting, Teddy.
TEDDY	No. This is mine. No women.
RACHEL	She doesn't mean just us. She means all of us here.
TEDDY	We don't need women involved in this political process.
ROBERT	What political process? What are you guys talking about?
RACHEL	We're gonna talk about what this reserve's gonna do now that there's no more fareWel.
ROBERT	What?

NIGGER	No fareWel cheques today. No happy day. It was sad day today.
TEDDY	You're not gonna talk about anything Rachel. You get the hell out of here.
RACHEL	No. Why don't you get the hell out of here Teddy. No one asked you to do this.
TEDDY	And no one asked you.
ROBERT	What are you doing? What are you guys talking about?

> *RACHEL and TEDDY speak at the same time.*

RACHEL	Teaching.
TEDDY	Self-government.

> *RACHEL and ROBERT speak at the same time.*

BOTH	What?
TEDDY	This is about self-government.
RACHEL	Whose self-government?
TEDDY	Ours. The Partridge Crop First Nation's.
MELVIN	This reserve?
TEDDY	It's a nation now. A new name for a new power.
PHYLLIS	You want to talk about self-government?
TEDDY	I'm gonna do it.
ROBERT	The chief isn't going to let you.
TEDDY	He doesn't care. If he did he would have got our cheques for us. Right? Right, Phyllis?

PHYLLIS	I dunno.
TEDDY	He's not even here.
ROBERT	Where is he?
ALL	(*save ROBERT*) He's in Vegas.
ROBERT	Oh. Nobody told me.
RACHEL	You can't have self-government here Teddy. No one wants it. They just want their welfare and parties.
TEDDY	That's what you want. I want a new future for our people.
RACHEL	And our people's money. How do you suppose to do this anyways?
TEDDY	We'll have nominations and then pick the chief. I call this meeting to order. You guys sit down.

> *RACHEL and ROBERT stand. MELVIN and PHYLLIS move to sit down. TEDDY stops PHYLLIS.*

TEDDY	Not you.
PHYLLIS	Why?
TEDDY	You're a woman.
RACHEL	So?
TEDDY	Go make food for Schmidty's wake.
RACHEL	Go make another baby.
TEDDY	Hey. We don't need you here.
ROBERT	You need everybody, Teddy.
TEDDY	Not women.

PHYLLIS	Let's go Rachel.
	PHYLLIS tries to move RACHEL. RACHEL doesn't move.
ROBERT	Let them stay Teddy. Future chiefs are fair.
TEDDY	Stay or go. I don't care. They don't get a vote. I call this meeting to order.
RACHEL	Who died and made you chief?
TEDDY	No one. Yet.
ROBERT	Are you the chair?
TEDDY	Yes.
NIGGER	Maybe he's a table.
TEDDY	Shut up, Nigger. Who nominates me?
ROBERT	Hold it Teddy. You should be chosen chair first. And someone has to second that nomination. But you should have the selection of chair first.
NIGGER	How come all this furniture?
TEDDY	That's white man's ways.
RACHEL	The whole thing you're doing is white man's ways. We never used to vote for chief.
TEDDY	And women weren't allowed.
ROBERT	Hold it. Hold it. You guys can't do this. You need to talk about this. Talk about it more.
RACHEL	Yes. Talk, then do something.
TEDDY	That's all we've been doing is talk. It's time to move.
ROBERT	You need to consult the elders. Like Sheldon here.

TEDDY

Who? Nigger? (*TEDDY starts laughing*)

RACHEL

Not consult. Teach. We need to ask them to teach us.

TEDDY

We need you to shut up.

PHYLLIS

We need help. Robert, help us.

ROBERT

I'd be wasting my time.

TEDDY

If that's what you think self-government is, get the hell out.

ROBERT waits and is about to leave.

MELVIN

You'd be a good chief, Robert.

TEDDY

Shut up you little asshole.

MELVIN

I'd even vote for you for free.

ROBERT stays.

ROBERT

Go ahead Teddy, nominate yourself.

TEDDY

I nominate myself chief of the Partridge Crop First Nation.

ROBERT

O.K. now someone has to second it, or else you can't stand.

NIGGER

Why? Does he have to sit down?

ROBERT

You. Melvin. Do you second Teddy for chief?

MELVIN

I do.

ROBERT

O.K. Well?

MELVIN

Well what?

ROBERT

Say, "I second Teddy for Chief."

MELVIN	Oh. I second Teddy for chief.
NIGGER	I third him.
ROBERT	You can't do that.
NIGGER	Why?
ROBERT	You don't have to. Now you have to have other nominations for the same position.
RACHEL	I nominate myself for chief.
TEDDY	You can't.
RACHEL	I just did.
MELVIN	I nominate Robert Traverse for chief.
RACHEL	Second me Phyllis.
NIGGER	I nominate me for chief.
PHYLLIS	I second Rachel for chief.
RACHEL	I second Robert for chief.
TEDDY	Stop.
ROBERT	Yes. Hold on. Thank you, but I don't want to be chief. Don't nominate me. I'm not standing.
NIGGER	Standing. Sitting. Chairs. Tables. First. Second. How come Robert knows so much. I bet just lying to us.
ROBERT	I'm not lying to you. You can look it up. The rules I'm using are called Robert's rules of order.
NIGGER	Aaaahhh. See. I knew it. These are his rules. He's just trying to get what he wants.
ROBERT	They're not mine.

NIGGER	Why are they called Robert's rules then?
ROBERT	I don't know. Because that's who wrote them.
NIGGER	Aaaahhh. He's lying. He wrote them.
ROBERT	I learned them doing community development for Indian Affairs.
NIGGER	He's lying.
TEDDY	Shut up, Nigger.
NIGGER	We're supposed to sing "O Canada" before our meeting or "God Save the Queen".
TEDDY & ROBERT	Shut up, Nigger.
NIGGER	(*singing*) O Canada. Our home and native land—(*he punches up 'native' for added effect*) A native person wrote that song.
MELVIN	That's not what it means.
NIGGER	Sure it does. Native. That's us right.
MELVIN	Yeah, but not like that.
NIGGER	I read a book. It said Canada is from Natives. It means "free land".
TEDDY	Shut up, you assholes. I disbar Robert as chief.
NIGGER	I second that.
PHYLLIS	You guys can't do that.
RACHEL	What a fuckin' joke. Robert's right. You don't even know what you're doing, Teddy.
TEDDY	At least I'm doing something.
RACHEL	Nobody asked you.

ROBERT   Hey. Hey. It doesn't matter. I'm not standing. I
                mean I'm not accepting the nomination for chief.
                So you have nothing to worry about.

MELVIN   Can you do that?

ROBERT   Yes.

MELVIN   Oh.

PHYLLIS   I nominate Melvin.

TEDDY
& RACHEL   I second.

TEDDY   I second him.

RACHEL   I do.

ROBERT   You guys. You guys. This isn't how you do it.

NIGGER   How do you know

ROBERT   Because I've been to meetings. I know how to do
                this. Be quiet. Look. Listen. You need a secretary.
                You need more people. You can't do this the way
                you're doing it. Planning. Preparation. You need all
                of these things. These things have to be thought
                out.

TEDDY   Why?

ROBERT   Ah hell, I'm leaving. You people are hopeless.

MELVIN   (*stopping him*) Wait. Robert you have to help us.
                You know the rules.

ROBERT   These guys aren't even listening to me. We can't do
                this. This doesn't mean anything.

TEDDY   Let him go.

MELVIN   Just stay.

ROBERT	There's no use. This isn't gonna work. We have to know what we're doing first.
MELVIN	Maybe. But still help us.
TEDDY	Stay or go. I don't give a shit. It's gonna happen without you.

MELVIN leads him back to a chair.

TEDDY	O.K., now we vote for chief.
ROBERT	The nominations have to be closed first.
MELVIN	What?
ROBERT	Never mind.
PHYLLIS	Wait. Wait. You have to give a speech.
TEDDY	Oh yeah. Let Melvin speak first.
MELVIN	I want Robert to speak for me.
PHYLLIS	Wait. Wait. I wanna pray first.
TEDDY	No.
PHYLLIS	Come on. I'm not nominated for anything. We need to pray first. Our people need God if we're gonna have self-government.
TEDDY	Our people need our own religion. Not that whiteman bullshit religion.
NIGGER	We need to sing "O Canada".

PHYLLIS starts to pray, eventually everyone except TEDDY and RACHEL bow their heads.

TEDDY	Fuckin' women.

PHYLLIS

Oh God, bless us in this thing we're doing, and don't let us be failures. And thank you for giving us Robert who can tell us what to do. And let our leaders be right and good for our people. Thank you Jesus. I don't know what self-government is, or what it's gonna be, but I pray you'll help us in it. Thank you, Jesus. And I'm sorry that we almost smoked your Bible and that nothing will happen to Rachel for that. Or to me. And don't let there be a number three. And bless Nigger, our elder, and Melvin, and Teddy. And Lord, maybe this isn't the time for us to have self-government, maybe we should wait for—

TEDDY

Amen.

RACHEL

Let her finish.

PHYLLIS

I'm finished. Amen. Jesus. Amen.

TEDDY

O.K. go and talk Melvin.

MELVIN

No.

ROBERT

Go on already.

MELVIN

Wait. I want Robert to talk first. I'm not gonna talk. I just want to hear what he has to say.

TEDDY

Ahhh shit. O.K. then. Let's get this over with. Robert's gonna talk first.

ROBERT

I don't wanna talk.

> *RACHEL holds onto the seat of her chair and begins hopping up and down with it, chanting "Talk". Soon, everyone else who is sitting joins in, until ROBERT rises, sits on the box and begins to talk.*

ROBERT

Listen. Self-government is something native people should have had long ago. Instead of begging for handouts. Whether it's for our schools

	or whatever. A lot of us who don't think we are, are really bums.
NIGGER	That's me. I was a bum on Main Street until that police car hit me and I got ten thousand dollars and I came home, and then I sobered up.
MELVIN	You never sobered up. You're still drunk.
ROBERT	I didn't mean you, Nigger. I was just trying to make a point. I'm sorry if I offended you.
NIGGER	No. That's O.K. I know who I am, and what I was. Just let me say something. The way I used to get money from people on the street was when I looked really pitiful. That's what you guys do when you go to Ottawa. Look really sad and they'll give you money. (*making a pitiful face*) Or else play music. Like a fiddle. I'm gonna take my fiddle and go back to Winnipeg and make money.
ROBERT	You asked me here for a meeting. A meeting on self-government. What is that? Can any of you tell me?
RACHEL	It's a different name for what we got now.
TEDDY	It's self-government. Just like the words mean. We govern ourselves. No more Indian Affairs.
ROBERT	O.K...and?
TEDDY	And...we get our own money. We get to look after ourselves.
RACHEL	You mean you get our money.
ROBERT	Rachel. Please. How much money is that, do you think?
TEDDY	A couple million.
ROBERT	Probably. Can you balance books?

TEDDY	Sure.
ROBERT	That wouldn't help you anyways. The Partridge Crop Reserve is broke. Their cheques all bounce. There's only one bank in Ashern that will cash welfare cheques and only welfare cheques. No other reserve cheques.
PHYLLIS	Teddy wouldn't even cash my little cheque.
TEDDY	Shut up, you.
ROBERT	Do you know what a ledger is? Or a balance sheet? Or how to do a payroll? Or calculate taxes?
TEDDY	We don't pay taxes.
ROBERT	Sure we do. We pay GST. Soon we'll be paying income tax too.
NIGGER	No way.
ROBERT	Yes we will. Who do you think pays for your happy day?
TEDDY	The government.
ROBERT	And who gives them money?
TEDDY	I don't know.
ROBERT	Taxpayers. They can't even pay for Medicare anymore. You think they're gonna care about a bunch of Indians?
TEDDY	They owe us.
ROBERT	I know they do. But you live on what they've given you. The land on this reserve is all we're ever gonna get. *This* reserve is less than a thousand square miles. And this country is millions of square miles. But this is all we're gonna get. And we're gonna get even less, as the money runs out.

TEDDY

We'll just take our land back.

MELVIN

We can't. We lost it. We're a defeated nation.

TEDDY

We're not a defeated nation. We never were. If they came here and kicked our asses instead of shaking our hands everything would have been fine. Then our people understood defeat. What it is to lose a war. And what that means. Instead we get tricked. And all this shit you see around you is because of that. They're still doing it. What do you think fareWel is?

ROBERT

We need self-determination. Not self-government. And. Within the current political system.

TEDDY

That's what we've had for the last hunerd years.

RACHEL

What Robert just tried to do is what we need. Teaching.

> *RACHEL walks up to and stands on the podium.*

TEDDY

Get off there.

RACHEL

We need teaching. We need to learn to live a different way. Not on welfare. We can't keep doing the same thing over and over. We're only gonna get one chance at self-government and we have to make it right.

TEDDY

Yeah. Good. O K

> *TEDDY tries to pull RACHEL off the podium.*

RACHEL

Let me finish. We need God too. If you want to believe Christian. Fine. If you want to believe Traditional. Fine. But we got to stop fighting each other all the time.

TEDDY

Yeah. (*TEDDY pulling her off the box*)

RACHEL	And we need to listen to each other. Teddy.

ROBERT starts to clap for RACHEL. The others join in, except TEDDY. ROBERT starts to leave.

PHYLLIS	Where are you going, Robert?
ROBERT	Home.
PHYLLIS	How come?
ROBERT	I've seen this one before.

ROBERT leaves.

TEDDY	O.K. Melvin it's your turn to get up there.

MELVIN sits, until TEDDY grabs him and puts him at the front. He does not stand on the box.

MELVIN	I don't know wannu.
TEDDY	Make your speech.
MELVIN	I don't know what a ledger is. And I didn't know our reserve was so small compared to the rest of Canada. Robert should be Chief. Not me. I don't even know why you voted me for Chief, because I can't be Chief. I'm from Dogtown. Even though I'm Bill C-31.
NIGGER	Anyone can be chief. Even a whiteman.
MELVIN	I'm not white. But I feel Indian.
RACHEL	It's what's in your heart.
MELVIN	I don't know what's in my heart.
TEDDY	Just shut up and finish your speech.

MELVIN	O.K. The only thing I know for sure is that nobody used to want to be chief. The Indian agent used to come and he would give the chief a new suit, and the councillors would get nothing.
NIGGER	That's right. I was a councillor for ten years.
MELVIN	The Chief worked free. Now that the Chief and council get paid. Everybody wants to be the Chief or on council. Maybe that's what we should have again. I shouldn't be chief anyways. I sniff.

TEDDY begins clapping, everyone but RACHEL joins in.

TEDDY	(*rising*) That was a good speech, Melvin.
RACHEL	Let him finish.
MELVIN	I'm finished.

TEDDY stands on the box.

TEDDY	Dih na way mahg a nay duk,
MELVIN	Wait, Teddy. Speak English.
TEDDY	Dih na way mahg a nay duk, asa wasa ki bi isha min ooma ka ai ing. Mi ooma ka dasi wo big ai ing. Ki kee asha dis oomin, shigo noong-um aa michi pee ang oki ma wi win chi meeni nang shoonian. A pee woogi mak an wi an ka ween shig o da ashan diki seem. Ka kin a awayish ta meena shoonian. Ki ka meeni ni nim shoonia. A way woogi mah kan ka ishad Las Vegas, pi san igoo mas kowi see win ki woo ta bi namin. A pee das ta gooshing ki ka sagichi way binanan, oomah woo chi ish koon i ganing. Ki ka machi a tad i minoma. Ka kina oono a tagaay wi nan ta pisco wheels of fortune, blackjack, shig oh slot machines. Mi ih kaa ishi shoonia kaa ing. Keena wind ki ga woono dah min away naan ki anishinabaywid. Ka ween a woshi may ongo blond hair ka ihwad, shi go ka away bawabi jee wabiwad Bill C-31 ka inid oh, ka

pi isha wad ki dish ko ni nan ing, ka pi woo da pin a wad ki shoonia min nin. Shi go ka iah way anishinabaa wit to win. Ki ka woo tabi min iway koy ak a nomiah win. Ka ween a wooshi may owoo way way miti goo ishi woo dana mi way igamik. Gakina Bazooka Joe anishinabaywid. (*holding up a Bazooka Joe comic*) Keena wah ka kin ah ki masi na a mak wim ka goo. Phyllis ki masi na a makwa shoonia. Nigger, ki masi na mow neen ka ki woo tabi na man ki wee bid.

NIGGER   Ka ween koosha ki kee wood tabi na seen ni wee wipid. Ka abi ni wee sa kaa dam.

TEDDY   Melvin ki masi na a maw-ka kee weegi nan chi aihin truck, ta goo gravel chi aihin ki meeka nang. Shig oh kaa keen Rachel ki masi na a mow chi pis nanabi ann, chi ki pa aman doon.

RACHEL kicks over an empty chair.

RACHEL   That's a lie.

MELVIN   What?

PHYLLIS   Rachel, don't.

TEDDY   Paa ka aka way hookerish.

RACHEL   I don't owe you anything. He says you owe him for that gravel on your Dad's road, Melvin.

MELVIN   What?

TEDDY   I got you that gravel. You wouldn't even have got any if it wasn't for me. You're a Bill C-31er.

MELVIN   I got that gravel. You didn't...I even asked before you and yet they gave everyone gravel except for me. That's how you can tell who's Bill C-31 on this reserve. They're the ones with dirt on their roads.

TEDDY   That's 'cause you're not pure.

MELVIN	I'm more Indian than you. (*TEDDY laughs*) In my heart. In my heart.
TEDDY	All you got is a card and some bullshit treaty number.
RACHEL	Teddy, you're not even pure yourself. Your granny was part white.
TEDDY	Woo nab in, pi sani apin.
RACHEL	You don't even know what you're doing here. This is a joke. Look at this fuckin' sign with your stupid face on it. (*RACHEL picks up one of the signs*) You look like a fuckin' dog.
TEDDY	Shut up.
RACHEL	We need teaching. That's the only way we're ever gonna get better.
TEDDY	Shut up.
RACHEL	No.
TEDDY	You shutup. Or I'll tell everyone what you are.
RACHEL	Go ahead. You're just as bad.
TEDDY	You know what this slut did?
RACHEL	He sleeps with hookers.
TEDDY	How would you know that?
RACHEL	Because. You were gonna sleep with me.
TEDDY	Yeah, right. One time in Winnipeg, I phone the hooker escort service and tell them to send me over a real pretty one, and this is what they send me.
RACHEL	You're just as bad. You sleep with hookers.

TEDDY   I sure as hell didn't want to sleep with you. I just laughed my head off.

RACHEL   You liar. You chased me down the hall. You wanted me so bad I could see your old pecker through your pants.

TEDDY   Ki ki chi ka wanim aki din.

RACHEL   Ka ween weeka ki da packi di na moosi noon. Why don't you go look after Margret and your baby, instead of making things worse for us.

TEDDY   (*grabbing RACHEL by the hair*) You whore bitch. You'd spread your legs for anyone with money eh? I would never sleep with you. (*releasing her*) She's not even proud of her own hair. Look at it. It's dyed. Indian hair. Black hair. She's embarrassed of it. It isn't even fuckin' clean.

NIGGER   That's enough.

TEDDY   Your damn right it's enough.

   TEDDY pushes RACHEL towards the door and kicks her in the rear.

   You get the hell off my reserve and get your black ass home.

   MELVIN sits, lost.

PHYLLIS   You're gonna get it, Teddy.

TEDDY   Maybe you're the one who's gonna get it, Phyllis.

   PHYLLIS helps RACHEL, and they both leave.

NIGGER   Why'd you do that, Teddy?

TEDDY   Shut up.

MELVIN   He's afraid of her.

TEDDY   Everyone shut the fuck up. Alright. Let's vote
              now. Who votes for Melvin? (*no one puts up their
              hand*) Who votes for me? (*TEDDY and NIGGER
              put up their hands*) Alright. Thank you. I accept
              your nomination as new chief. I will serve you
              good. Amen.

                            ***

Man You Mus'

Bianca Jacob

Bianca Jacob is a journalist, free-lance editor, arts administrator and producer — but always a playwright. Her first play - "Man You Mus'" - was one of three finalists (full-length category) in Theatre British Columbia's National Playwriting Competition. It was produced by Theatre International and Paul Robeson Theatre in New York on four occasions. Since then, Bianca has written "Sell-Out", "Mother-in-Law", and "Dream State" — all of which have been produced. Her journalistic writing has been featured in several publications over the past eight years. Bianca is also the artistic producer for Theatre People, a company she founded in 1991 to explore the Canadian-Caribbean theatre aesthetic.

Man You Mus'

Bianca Jacob

*Act One, Scene One establishes the relationship
between Jean, Gloria, and Kemba and gives a peep into
village politics and small-place gossip. This scene also
establishes the character of Jean who is a nice, good
church girl and Gloria who is somewhat of a vamp. We
also learn about Pernel who is apparently trying to
swindle Jean — his fiancée.*

> *A backyard in a small village in Trinidad. Two
> modest houses one to the front right of the
> yard and the other in the background. JEAN is
> sitting on a bench, washing in a tub. She gets
> up to hang the clothes on the clothes line, then
> returns to her seat. Eight year old KEMBA
> comes out of her house and watches JEAN,
> then she creeps up behind her and places her
> fingers around her eyes.*

KEMBA   Guess who it is?

JEAN   Kemba what is wrong with you?

KEMBA   Miss Jean, Mammy say if you have a pinch of salt
to lend her please?

JEAN   Your mother still home?

KEMBA   Yes.

JEAN	Go inside and look on the shelf, you will see the salt in a bottle mark curry, carry the whole bottle. Kemba how come you didn't go to Sabbath school today?
KEMBA	Because my church dress dirty.
JEAN	That is two Sundays you haven't been to church, you can't put God second you know.
KEMBA	Miss Jean I could go for the salt now?
JEAN	O.K. and tell your mother don't forget the address.
KEMBA	(*giggles*) Yes.
JEAN	Yes who?
KEMBA	Yes, Miss Jean.

KEMBA exits, then her mother, GLORIA, enters.

GLORIA	Kemba? Where is this child?
JEAN	She gone for the salt. Well, good morning.
GLORIA	Morning Jean, I better let you do my laundry too.
JEAN	If you didn't use to keep so much late nights you would be able to wash your own clothes, instead of throwing them away. You would be able to buy your own salt too.
GLORIA	(*laughs*) You like to give you mouth too much liberties.
JEAN	I giving my mouth liberties? Kemba just tell me that her church dress dirty. And meanwhile you coming home with a strange man at 4:17 this morning.
GLORIA	(*sarcastically*) You sure you have the time right?

JEAN　　　　Look I wasn't trying to mind your business you know, I just wanted...

GLORIA　　　You just wanted to know. One of these days someone will spit in your eyes while you peeping through the curtains. And I will be right there to laugh, if I wasn't the one who spit to begin with.

JEAN　　　　Gloria don't forget. That is you and not me is the village maco.

GLORIA　　　Please, Jean, not because you are a church girl, mean that you have to give me that holier than thou attitude. We know each other too long for that.

JEAN　　　　Gloria, you know I don't like it when you bring de church into your conversation. Look, if you don't want to tell me about the company you keeping is all right.

GLORIA　　　If you must know that is Mr. Bishop the new doctor that take over from stupid Francis down at the health centre.

JEAN　　　　You weren't calling him stupid Francis when he just moved into the village though. But, how you and Mr. Bishop get so close? I mean the man just move into the village yesterday morning.

GLORIA　　　You think I have time to wait for them destitute women in this backyard to get home?

JEAN　　　　Gloria, what is your secret, why men so crazy about you? I mean you only average looking.

GLORIA　　　Me? I Average looking? Ah sweet looking speciman like me.

JEAN　　　　I hear that you don't rely on your sweetness alone. Villagers say you use obeah to take other people's husband. Tell me, that is true?

GLORIA   How come you talking about obeah, I thought you are ah church girl.

JEAN   Where there is good there must be evil.

GLORIA   Jean, since we high so, me and you are friends, you mean you listening to village gossip about me too?

JEAN   Look Gloria, I just wanted you to know what people saying about you.

GLORIA   Don't listen to them is only jealousy have them talking so, I don't need obeah I have my ways to do things.

JEAN   What kind of ways?

GLORIA   I operate by one main philosophy...women vindictive and men stupid. Once you understand that you win the battle.

JEAN   What battle you talking?

GLORIA   The battle of the sexes. Men always feel they have the upper hand, let them believe that and yuh win.

JEAN   I eh follow you.

GLORIA   Look when you meet ah fella is three things you check out, his bank account, his marital status, and the way AIDS spreading these days don't forget his sexual history. Once you satisfied you plan the attack.

JEAN   Attack?

GLORIA   Find out what he likes in a woman and that is the woman you must become.

JEAN   But that is deceitfulness? I would never do that.

GLORIA   Jean don't be so judgmental, sometimes you have to force somebody hand to get what you want.

JEAN   Not me, I rather lose than resort to trickery and manipulation.

GLORIA   Then why you questioning me?

JEAN   I not interested but I could see that you need to talk about it.

GLORIA   Listen well, first learn how to cook. My wise old mother say the way to a man's heart is through his stomach.

JEAN   What else she tell you?

GLORIA   I thought you didn't want to know. Just feed him good, do what he say and everything will fall into place.

JEAN   And what if you don't agree with what he say?

GLORIA   Do it anyway, cause once you get the ring on the second finger of your left hand you could do as you please.

KEMBA   (*has been listening quietly, unobserved*) Mammy if you have so much strategy why you still single?

GLORIA   Kemba, was me and Miss Jean talking to you?

KEMBA   No Ma, but if you ask me the way you talking I should have a daddy by now and furthermore...

GLORIA   And furthermore find yuh little tail inside or ah will blaze yuh with licks.

KEMBA   But Ma...

GLORIA   Now (*chasing KEMBA to the house*) these children they making these days too damn fresh.

JEAN   Well you know what de Bible say the little children shall lead them. But Kemba ask a good question how come you still by yourself and you know so much about men?

GLORIA   Well I meet a few that would do me just fine. But they not the kind of example I want for Kemba.

JEAN   She growing up nice but ah child does really need a father. Don't worry Gloria you will get ah good man.

GLORIA   I'm beginning to think there is no such thing as a good man.

JEAN   Pernel is ah good man.

GLORIA   If Pernel is ah good man I change meh name.

JEAN   Gloria how you could say that?

GLORIA   If he so good, why he only come to see you once, since he come from Canada.

JEAN   He's been very busy.

GLORIA   Too busy to spend time with a fiancée he hasn't seen in three years?

JEAN   Is not only me he have living in Trinidad, he have his friends to see too.

GLORIA   It don't bother you that his friends come before you?

JEAN   Why it should bother me? I know when I go to live in Canada with Pernel everything will be fine.

GLORIA   And when exactly is that?

JEAN   When things with the house we buying finalise, I just have to give him the last set of money when he going back and...

GLORIA   How come you always sending your hard earn dollars to Pernel?

JEAN	They call that woman's lib, and liberation means that I have to pull my weight.
GLORIA	So tell me how much you give him so far?
JEAN	About 10,000 dollars
GLORIA	Trinidad and Tobago dollars?
JEAN	No.
GLORIA	Canadian dollars?
JEAN	You have a problem with that?
GLORIA	Jean you do understand that every Canadian dollar is worth four, five of we currency?
JEAN	Why yuh getting on so? Pernel say that is just a drop in the bucket for a future homeowner.
GLORIA	Ah drop? Girl where I come from $10,000 is ah big splash.
JEAN	Look Pernel know what he doing.
GLORIA	I don't doubt that.
JEAN	I trust his judgement.
GLORIA	I trust his judgement too.
JEAN	I know what you thinking but I will leave you rotting right here in this stinking little village, and go and live with my future husband. Pernel loves me. Can you say the same for any man in your life?
GLORIA	Look Jean, I'm sorry, I had no right to say those things.
JEAN	Well if you want this friendship to continue keep your comments to yourself.

	A voice is heard singing a calypso as he makes his way through the yard. JACKO, an on duty postman, comes towards Jean and Gloria. He senses the tension between the women.
JACKO	What happening, Sis? (*kissing GLORIA*) Ah boy, Jean you looking hmmm.
JEAN	Gloria, look just tell your brother to leave me alone.
GLORIA	Don't get me involved in the two of you business. Since we small Jacko eyeing you.
JEAN	And is since then I telling him I am not interested.
GLORIA	Jean don't be so hard on him, look how he feeling shame.
JEAN	Jacko have no shame and no conscience.
JACKO	I wonder if Pernel appreciates what he have? I know if you was my woman (*whispering in her ear*).
JEAN	(*giggles*) Jacko!
JACKO	Ah serious, you know.
JEAN	Like you does forget that Pernel is your best friend, you have no morality.
JACKO	And I don't want none. You know what I want.
GLORIA	Jacko that is enough, leave Jean alone.
JACKO	I know I don't have a good reputation around here, but ah nice church girl like Jean could make a respectable man out of me. Here one for you. They say they will cut your lights if you don't pay your bill tomorrow.
GLORIA	Give me that.

JACKO	And darling this one for you. It come from foreign from somebody name Sherry Bouzoon. Who is that? I hold it up to the sun, but the envelope so thick ah can't make out a thing.
JEAN	Jacko why you so fast?
JACKO	I was just trying to help. Some people so uptight. I could fix that you know.
JEAN	Go nah.
JACKO	O.K., ah leaving but one day you will beg me to come back, and you know what?
JEAN	What?
JACKO	Ah will come.

JACKO exits, but his voice is heard as he makes his rounds.

Miss Mabel, your pension cheque come. Mr. George, the day of reckoning is here — Princess taking you to court, I have the summons right here.

GLORIA	Who the letter from? The person have the same surname like Pernel.
JEAN	I going inside, I will talk to you later.
GLORIA	But you could read it right here. Oh gosh Jean please...

JEAN enters her house, and closes the door leaving Gloria on the step, who positions herself to listen.

GLORIA	I don't know why she just didn't tell me and save me this discomfort.

JEAN	"Dear Jean, This letter is long overdue, I want to thank you for your generous gift. The reason I haven't written before is Pernel said that you don't like to be thanked. He said you are so rich that you get pleasure from giving away your money. Pernel is very lucky to have a sister like you. He told me how close you two were when you were growing up. He said that your mother would have loved me if she were alive. I want you to know that since Pernel and I got married we have been very happy. We have also made good use of the money you gave us. We bought a house in a place known as Brampton. It's beautiful. I hope you will visit us one day. I remain your sister-in-law, Sherry Bouzoon."
JEAN	Oh God what this mean...Gloria (*as she opens the door GLORIA falls in*) Here read this.
GLORIA	Is O.K. I hear everything. Clever! The man brilliant. First off...he take yuh money and buy house. Secondly, he got married to somebody who is not you. I was wondering how come he don't have Canadian papers and he travelling. Oh, so he wife sponsor him. The man smart.
JEAN	It must be a mistake, somebody trying to break up me and Pernel.
GLORIA	Wake-up girl, can't you see he even cover he track by telling his wife you are his sister.
JEAN	Stop calling that woman his wife.
GLORIA	Wife, wife, wife. She is his wife, he is she husband. They are married, that proves my point.
JEAN	What point?

GLORIA	That it have no good man again. Where yuh going? Jean come back. I sure is Pernel she gone by. Hmmm, women vindictive and man stupid, or maybe is man vindictive, stupid and wicked too.

*

> *Act One, Scene Three. The cemetery, complete with noise of the night. GLORIA is crouched behind a tombstone - this is her idea. JEAN is looking for her when they bump into each other, screaming.*

GLORIA	Jean, you frighten me.
JEAN	Gloria is you? I should have never let you talk me into coming here.
GLORIA	Shhh, you insulting the spirits!
JEAN	What sprits?
GLORIA	You not feeling all the spirits of the dead people in the village? If you want them to help you, you have to say good things, Dear, dead Ms. Maple, you know I had always thought you were a bitch when you were alive, but is not me who need you help — is Jean and she never thought that you were a bitch.
JEAN	If you trying to make me feel better, it eh working.
GLORIA	You bring the things I tell you to bring? I have the first milk of a morning goat, the manicou and the eye of a common fowl.
JEAN	And I have the middle tow of a crapud, the bottle of rum, and three grains of Pernel hair, two grey, you think that matters?
GLORIA	That should be all right man, but how you get the hair?

JEAN	I phone and told his mother, what Pernel do to me and what I was going to do to him and she personally plucked it from his head while he was sleeping.
GLORIA	And they say mothers worship their sons.
JEAN	I don't understand the family politics between them but thanks to she I get the hair.
GLORIA	You bring the money too?
JEAN	Girl, the bank was closed so I had to borrow the money from Jacko. He so fas' he want to know what it for.
GLORIA	You didn't tell him though?
JEAN	Ah smarter than that.
GLORIA	I hope you bring the whole 300 dollars, de man don't take short money.
JEAN	For the price he charging he better be damn good.

A frightening and very loud drum call is heard, the women grab on to each other, and an apparition jumps out of the darkness.

OBEAHMAN   Who troubles the spirits at twelve in the morn.
Whilst the duppy foam, and the dwens are born
When Soucouyant's attire,
Is a ball of fire,
And the laghoo rides in the dead of 'night,
Sucking blood with all his might.
And I am cemetery in obeah I delve.

When the smoke clears GLORIA and JEAN are standing before the OBEAHMAN.

What is you desire? Oh ho Gloria is you, I guess you hear to trap another poor man.

JEAN   So is true.

GLORIA	No he just joking. I come here with Jean she is the one with problem.
OBEAHMAN	I hope you tell she to bring my pay.
JEAN	Yes I bring it, hurry up obeahman.
OBEAHMAN	Don't call me that! I am a man of medicine, you suppose to call me doctor. Long ago ah man like me was important. Today, allyuh have like ah pappyshow, quick to say that obeah not real, but as soon as you in problem, everybody come running.
GLORIA	How come you so talkative tonight, we want to leave this cemetery man.
JEAN	Yes just say if you could help or not.
OBEAHMAN	That depends.
JEAN	On what?
OBEAHMAN	You bring the manicou, the fowl eye, the middle toe of a crapaud, ah bottle of rum, the first milk of the morning goat?
JEAN	Yes, Miss Experienced Gloria tell me what to bring.
OBEAHMAN	Now put my money on that tombstone dey. Now we could commence Gloria, you go and wait for Jean somewhere else, you have them spirits and dem too restless.
GLORIA	Jean meet me by the taxi-stand when you done. You know something you looking ah little taller tonight.
OBEAHMAN	That is because of the power that is bestowed upon me at midnight.

GLORIA exists, he watches her go.

Come closer Jean, you ever heard about 'Man You Mus'?

JEAN   Man You Mus'?

OBEAHMAN   It is an old African potion I could promise you, that if you give ah man to drink he must do whatever you tell him too.

JEAN   Whatever?

OBEAHMAN   Anything.

JEAN   That is exactly what I looking for.

OBEAHMAN   We will mix a strong dosage, so we will finish Pernel in one shot. I will stir in the hair with the milk.

JEAN   What about the manicou and the rum? Put that in here too?

OBEAHMAN   You mad or what? The manicou and the rum is for a special sacrifice I have to perform for myself later.

JEAN   You sure this will work?

OBEAHMAN   Say what in yuh heart.

JEAN   Pernel is ah nasty son of ah b...

OBEAHMAN   No! I mean say what you want the potion to do.

JEAN   Wherever you go Pernel, Man You Mus' must reach. One drink, one dose, and you will think how I want you to think, do what I want you to do. My Man You Mus' will teach you a lesson.

OBEAHMAN   Well said...you sure this is your first time?

JEAN   (*grabbing the stick*) Yes and I tell you that. I only here because that man push me beyond my limits. Stir that thing Obeahman, stir it good.

OBEAHMAN   I really sorry to hear that, is ah tragedy to see what does come after de love done. Just put ah drop in anything he drinking.

JEAN   This better work you know.

JEAN runs out of the cemetery.

OBEAHMAN   How it could work? (*taking off his mask, it is PERNEL*) How I could do that to myself? Is ah lucky thing meh mother warn me about Jean plans. Well $50 for Mammy, the rest is mine. Well let me go and rounds up Jacko and the boys and cook this rat and drink this Vat. Jean eh no match for me. Jacko, Niko is me Pernel we have ah cook tonight.

***

Noran Bang: The Yellow Room

M.J. Kang

Myung Jin Kang is a playwright and writer based in Toronto. Her plays include "Noran Bang: The Yellow Room", the collective creation - "Urban Donnellys", and "My Sister's Visit". Her work has been published in *Fireweed*, *Diva* magazine, and the Playwrights Canada Press anthology, *Taking the Stage - Selections from Plays by Canadian Women*.

She has been a part of the Tarragon Theatre / Chalmers Playwrights Unit as playwright in residence at Cahoots Theatre Projects. The premiere of her newest play, "Blessings", is scheduled for production at Tarragon Theatre in 1996.

Noran Bang: The Yellow Room

M.J. Kang

The death of Halmonee (grandmother) in Korea ignites a wave of explosive emotional confrontations within a Korean-Canadian family. Umma (mother) begs for permission to return to her homeland and pay her respects. Apba (father), preoccupied with the need to improve his family's material standing, dismisses this request as extravagance. The two young daughters, Gyung-June and Mee-Gyung, are forced to survive on their own terms, even as forces threaten to divide them.

The "present" time of the play is the late 1970's. The lives of the Korean family in Toronto are affected not only by the immigration experience in Canada, but by present, past, and personal events in Korea. Dream, memory, and politics are braided together, with Korean dance, drumming, and slide images, to evoke theatrically the culturally hybrid experience of Koreans in Canada.

	Scene One. UMMA is sitting by the kitchen table, holding a picture of HALMONEE, crying. MEE-GYUNG enters, confused. It is in the middle of the night. All is silent except the terrible weeping. MEE-GYUNG appears slowly, almost hesitantly.
MEE-GYUNG	Umma? Umma. I'm sorry. Umma? Umma! *(starting to cry)* Umma! Umma!
UMMA	Halmonee. Halmonee chew-g-saw. Halmonee chew-g-saw! (Grandmother. Grandmother passed away. Grandmother passed away.)

GYUNG-JUNE enters as if in a trance.

GYUNG-JUNE	Umma. I had a dream. Grandmother is dead. We were in a battlefield and she gave me a red flower. Everything else was black and white. She kissed me with a blood flower and told me to be strong. Then she walked along a line — a white line on the ground to a farm. The farm was on the line. Her hair shed to the ground and her clothes became full of bullets. I couldn't kiss her. I was holding on to her but I wasn't touching her. I couldn't. She flew me a rose. A white rose and told me to love this country. Love this country. She wants to hold me, Umma. She can't die unless I hold her.
UMMA	It's too late, Gyung-June.
GYUNG-JUNE	I don't believe you.
UMMA	Moo-sum mah ri-ah! (What talk is that!)
GYUNG-JUNE	Bring me back, just bring me back.
MEE-GYUNG	Grandmother's dead? Where is she?
UMMA	In Korea.
GYUNG-JUNE	I want to go back!
MEE-GYUNG	Korea?
GYUNG-JUNE	I need to go back to Korea!
APBA	Dang shin.
UMMA	Your father is calling me.
GUNG-JUNE	Please.
APBA	Come here.
UMMA	Be quiet, before he gets angered.

GYUNG-JUNE	I'm going back! To be with Halmonee. She's not dead. I can feel her, Umma. She's waiting for me.
UMMA	He won't let me go back. He tells me we have no money, no money to see my mother buried. No money to go anywhere.
APBA	Stupid wife, come here. Now!
GYUNG-JUNE	I hate it here!
UMMA	(*hitting GYUNG-JUNE*) Stop being selfish, ugly child!

UMMA exits.

MEE-GYUNG	Cah, why'd she hit you?

Pause.

GYUNG-JUNE	Grandmother is dead.

***

Scene Two. In the bedroom of UMMA and APBA.

APBA	Dang shin, stop crying. Crying doesn't help. Come back to bed. (*passing her a roll of toilet paper*) Here.
UMMA	Am I supposed to shit my tears? (*pause*) Look at what we've lost.
APBA	(*trying to console her*) It was a matter of survival.
UMMA	We had a good life in Korea. We had a home. And we had family. And we were happy.
APBA	No more talk. Time to go to bed. It's late!
UMMA	(*simultaneously*) But you told me to pack my things and travel, travel to this, this place!

APBA   (*simultaneously*) Time to go to bed. It's late!

Sang-nim kee-gee-bau! (*as UMMA lies down beside him with her back to him*) Sleep well.

***

Scene Three. In MEE-GYUNG's and GYUNG-JUNE's bedroom. GYUNG-JUNE is crying. MEE-GYUNG is staring at the ceiling.

MEE-GYUNG   Cah, what happened tonight?

GYUNG-JUNE   You don't remember anything about Korea, do you? You don't even remember Halmonee!

MEE-GYUNG   No.

GYUNG-JUNE   Then why were you crying?

MEE-GYUNG   I don't know. Umma was crying.

GYUNG-JUNE   Umma was crying. Halmonee promised to be with me. Mee-Gyung, she can't die unless I'm with her.

MEE-GYUNG   Am I bad for not remembering?

GYUNG-JUNE   No. You were so young when we left. Everyone loved you because you were so quiet. Not as loud as our cousin. Do you remember Hyuck-Donn?

HYUCK-DONN is a young boy of about nine years. He is in the yard of a small house in Korea.

HYUCK-DONN   Sit down. I said, 'Sit!' Lazy dog! (*whacking the ground with a wooden stick*)

WHITE DOG is an oldish, grumpy sort of dog who looks like he has lived a few too many years. He barks.

Listen to me!

GYUNG-JUNE   He annoyed everyone and kept on trying to take my
                    dog. But the dog was very smart, Mee-Gyung.
                    Never, ever listened to a word Hyuck-Donn spoke.

HYUCK-DONN   (*prodding WHITE DOG with a stick*) I'll poke you
                    until you sit. Do you like being poked?

WHITE DOG   I hate you, you little jerk.

GYUNG-JUNE   Remember the dog I had?

MEE-GYUNG   The big white one, Cah?

GYUNG-JUNE   Yes. The big white one. White Dog.

HYUCK-DONN   (*whacking the ground with a stick*) Why are you
                    barking so? I'm not scared by you! Sit down! I said,
                    'Sit down!'

                    WHITE DOG growls.

GYUNG-JUNE   (*exiting from small house*) Hyuck-Donn! Leave
                    him alone!

WHITE-DOG   (*to GYUNG-JUNE*) Just let me bite him. Right
                    on his bum.

                    GYUNG-JUNE laughs.

HYUCK-DONN   What's he saying? How come you can understand
                    him?

WHITE-DOG   One little bite. Right there. Left cheek. Bulls eye!

GYUNG-JUNE   Be nice, he's my cousin. (*to HYUCK-DONN*) Why
                    is my dog angered?

HYUCK-DONN   Because he's stupid!

                    WHITE DOG growls.

GYUNG-JUNE   (*to HYUCK-DONN*) What have you been doing to
                    him?

HYUCK-DONN	Nothing. That dog is stupid. He can't respect that I am smarter! Why do you get the dog all the time?
GYUNG-JUNE	Because I am smarter. And my dog is smarter than you too.
WHITE-DOG	Tell him, Gyung-June!

HALMONEE enters without being noticed.

GYUNG-JUNE	My dog is smart enough to know you are a bad person. A bad person he shouldn't play with. He's not allowed to play with.
HYUCK-DONN	What do you mean, not allowed to play with?
GYUNG-JUNE	I said so.
WHITE DOG	Oh, oh.
HYUCK-DONN	Your mother said I can play with him whenever I want. He's not just your dog, but mine too. Your mother said I can have anything of yours because we're cousins.
GYUNG-JUNE	He's my dog!
HALMONEE	Shi-ku-ro! If grandfather catches you fighting again, neither of you will be invited back.
GYUNG-JUNE	Halmonee, Hyuck-Donn tried to kill my dog!
HALMONEE	Now Gyung-June, everything will be okay. You've been fighting too hard. Come inside and have yummy ducc gouk.
GYUNG-JUNE	And you put some mandu too?
HALMONEE	Yes, special pork dumplings made fresh today. For my only Gyung-June. (*to HYUCK-DONN*) Hyuck-Donn, you can eat after you've finished tying up the dog and taking a bath. Ahh-u! Nem-say-nah! (My God, how smelly!) (*to GYUNG-JUNE*) Come inside now, Gyung-June-ee.

> *HALMONEE and GYUNG-JUNE exit.*

WHITE-DOG Steal some mandu for me, okay, Gyung-June?

> *HYUCK-DONN drags WHITE DOG to be tied.*

GYUNG-JUNE (*to MEE-GYUNG who has fallen asleep*) That's how grandmother was. Even when I wasn't the saint, she took my side.

***

Sliding for Home

Jean Yoon

Jean Yoon is a poet, playwright, theatre artist and reluctant arts administrator living in Toronto. She has served as Cross-Cultural Co-ordinator at Theatre Ontario, and as Co-Artistic Director of Cahoots Theatre Projects. She is currently President of the Board of Cahoots and a freelance artist. Her poems and short stories have been published in various magazines and anthologies including *Fireweed, what, muae,* and *Premonitions: The Kaya Anthology of New Asian North American Poetry.*

Sliding for Home

by Jean Yoon

A young Korean-Canadian woman returns to Korea for the first time, only to be 'held hostage' by her relatives. There's nothing to watch on television but The Family Reunification Program and baseball.

This play was first performed as a monologue, and has also been performed by a cast of three: with one actor playing Jean , animating the television voices - Mr. Han and Miss Kim; a second actor plays Grandmother, Cousin, Woman 1; and a third actor plays the Aunt and Woman 2.

The Korean national anthem sung awkwardly, as if being learned. A Korean flag gently unfurled. Lights up on JEAN, a less than demure Korean-Canadian woman.

JEAN   Seoul. Korea. It's 1983 and I'm here to learn about my culture. The only problem is, I can't get out of the house. I'm being held hostage by my relatives.

There's my grandfather:

GRANDFATHER   (*bossy Korean know-it-all-patriarch*) Hangook-ae-so nappun saram mannae-yoh. Cholmun yoja-ae-kae nomoo wee-hom ha-da!

JEAN   (*defiant*) Yeah, well, it's dangerous in Toronto too. And it's not like I'm a baby. I'm nineteen.

There's my grandmother:

GRANDMOTHER   (*bent over, ancient, slow, succouring*) Ol-kool
chom bo-jah, oo-ri sarang-ha-neun Jean-ee ol-kool
chom bo-jah. Ee-ru-wah! Ee-ru-wah, Jean-ee-yah...

JEAN   (*loving*) She's so sweet...

And of course there's my aunt:

AUNT   (*bubbly, chatty, excited*) Bakae-so ka-gee maa!
Tele-bi chom bwa! Telebi-chom bwa! Aie no-moo
chae-me-soh-yoh!

JEAN   (*bored and disgusted*) Telebi! TV. Get up. Watch
TV. Eat. Sleep. Watch TV. Sleep. I hate it here. I
want to go home.

There's the American channel:

   *JEAN clicks the remote control, turning on the
   TV: A southern American drawl.*

TV   In Pusan, the weather continues hot and muggy
with a high of 32 degrees. Thunderstorms predicted
for—

   *She clicks again. A commerical for Maxwell
   House. Sweet, sugary voice.*

TV   Achim ae pi-gon ha-say-yoh? (*bringing out a cup
and saucer*) Ko-pi chom teu-ship she-yoh! (*holding
up a Korean bottle of Maxwell House*) Maek-seu-
werl Ha-oo-seu! Mikook chae-il cho-oon Ko-pi im-
ni-da! (*sipping from the cup and letting out a sigh
of satisfaction*) Kut-ga-gee ma-shee-soh-yoh!

   JEAN clicks the TV off.

JEAN   My Korean might be bad but I know what she's
saying. So what's left? The Family Reunification
Program and Baseball.
The Family Reunification Program. There's
something you have to know. I mean, reunification

is the Korean National Dream. It's bigger than a
railway. More important than God. I mean, who
started the Reunification Church? Reverend Moon.
A Korean. Of course.

All Koreans everywhere yearn for it. I mean, we're
talking *families*, love, duty, belonging. In 1945,
Korea was divided, split in half like a watermelon;
families wrenched apart. Some in the South, some
in the North, some stuck in China — now we're
everywhere, New York, LA, San
Francisco...Toronto. And in all the confusion,
thousands of people lost contact with family *within
the borders*.

So the TV station starts this show.

An army of people camp out in front of the station,
all holding up placards with the name, age,
description of the brother, sister, mother, husband
lost in the war.

The camera pans the crowd, slowly so that you can
read all the placards, study all the faces.

A phone number flashes at the bottom of the
screen.

And then its:

MR. HAN

(*macho Korean TV host*) I think we have a match
up, isn't that right Miss Kim?

MISS KIM

(*sugary sweet Korean TV hostess*) Yes, that's right
Mr. Han. Mrs. Cho was separated from her younger
sister during their escape from Inchon. A caller
matching the description is in the station now. It's
so exciting, isn't it Mr. Han?

MR. HAN

It sure is!

JEAN

Split screen. Two women in their fifties. They
look exactly alike.

1ST WOMAN	(*on the phone, nervous*) Yobo-say-yoh?
2ND WOMAN	Yeah? Yobo-say-yoh?
1ST WOMAN	Tell me, this might seem like a silly question, but do you happen to have a small, a small, purple birthmark on your right shoulder?
2ND WOMAN	(*looking at her shoulder, shocked*) Yes! Yes, I do!
1ST WOMAN	And, and, how m-m-many siblings did you have?
2ND WOMAN	I had one older sister named Hae-Jong and an older brother named Yong-seu.
1ST WOMAN	Oh-mo-na! And how did you lose them?
2ND WOMAN	There was a fire, and we all ran out. There were planes and we were running and I tripped and—
1ST WOMAN	I let go of your hand! Oh Eun-Gee! Eun-Gee you're alive! Oh Eungee!
2ND WOMAN	On-ni,

> *There is a loud and confused flailing of arms, wailing, pulling of hair, as they beat themselves, and collapse to the floor.*

MISS KIM	It must be quite a thrill to be reunited with your sister after thirty years? (*aiming the mike at the floor where the women are wailing hysterically*)
WOMEN	Wahhh!
MR. HAN	It must be like a dream come true!
WOMEN	WAHHH!
MR. HAN	Well there you have it, ladies and gentlemen. Another happy reunification on KBS. Join us again tomorrow when—

> *JEAN clicks the TV off and stares stunned at the audience.*

JEAN

This is serious stuff. I mean, it's really moving. I'm gaining a whole new perspective on my culture. I could watch this all day. And I do. All day. Every day.

My family starts to get worried. They start saying I should go out once in a while. Get some air. They plan outings for me. My aunt *drags* me out shopping with her. But it's okay. The whole country is tuned into the Family Reunification Program. It's on in all the restaurants, ta-bangs, all the TVs in shop windows and department stores are turned on to the Family Reunification Program.

My aunt says:

AUNT

Have you noticed that the people who are looking are getting poorer and poorer.

JEAN

(*surprised*) It's true. I hadn't noticed.

AUNT

Look at their eyes. Hungry eyes. They're hoping to find rich relatives who will lend them money, help get them a better job.

JEAN

My grandmother says:

GRANDMOTHER

Ah-ni, ma-um sok-ae wae-roh-woh-yoh, keu-reu kae...

JEAN

And I think. Yeah! That's what it is — loneliness, grief...And my cousin says:

COUSIN

Baseball!

JEAN   Baseball. I'm a hockey girl, myself. I grew up
watching the Maple Leafs — not that it ever paid
off — but baseball is okay. (*JEAN and COUSIN
watch baseball*) It's non-territorial, team-oriented, a
linear kind of mind-set. First base, second base,
third base — I can get into this. And oh wow!
(*smitten*) There's Kim Pa-wee! Rocky Kim, sex
god and first baseman. He lifts a bat, shifts his
hips, taps his bat a few times, spits, and stares
boldly into the pitcher's eyes — (*stopping, then
pulling back*) You know, I'd swear, he, oh this is
freaky, he looks like, just like, he looks just
like — I gotta talk to my aunt...

        Kun om-monee, cho-gi Kim Pa-wee-ka oo-ri kajok
wa kachee, talmagee-yoh?

AUNT   Jeannie michyo-soh!

COUSIN   What are you saying, he doesn't look at all like us.

JEAN   (*to audience*) But he does. Look. (*pulling out a
picture of a Korean baseball player*) This is Kim
Pa-wee. You see the resemblance. (*pulling out
another photo, passport-style of the fifties — the
same man*) This is my Dad. You can see the
resemblance! I mean, he's probably a long lost
little brother who was separated from the family in
the rush from Seoul. A dark secret nobody wants to
talk about because that would mean—

GRANDFATHER (*screaming*) Shik-oori-wo-yoh!

JEAN   I didn't mean to suggest, Halabogee, I mean, I was
just, I'll shut up now...

        I watch baseball obesessively. (*clicking channels*) I
flip between baseball and the Family Reunification
program, baseball, reunification, baseball: Kim Pa-
wee is coming up to bat, the pitcher breaks, an
easy hit. And Kim Pa-wee wacks the ball far into
the outfield, a fumble, and Kim is racing for first
base!

JEAN   And people are crying, on their feet, hugging each other, wailing, hundreds of people screaming, cheering, waaaahhh!

Kim Pa-wee is rounding second, the outfielder tears the ball to the pitcher. But Kim Pa-wee is safe on third, he's running, he's racing to beat the ball, he's going for home—

Waahhhhh! Thirty years, thirty years, and now you're back, you're back, you're home—

And the pitcher blasts the ball to the catcher and Kim Pa-Wee is going for it, he's sliding for home! Kim Pa-wee is sliding for home! Safe! Safe! Kim Pa-wee makes it home!...Home.... Home.

I write letters to Kim Pa-wee in my pathetically elementary Korean. He does not write back. I get tickets for a game and can bearly see him. My family tells me to stop being silly, I'm just not used to seeing Korean faces. I dream about Kim Pa-wee, dreams which make me hope he's not really related because I am, we are, well....uhm. I mean he's a very sexy guy.

She kisses the photograph and puts it away.

The summer ends.

Sound effects of an airport announcer in Korean and then English.

At the airport everyone is crying, including me. My grandmother, my aunt and uncle, my cousins. I shake hands with my grandfather who tells me not to play goh if I am serious about being a writer. I wave goodbye to my sexist, male chauvinist cousin who after all is only the product of his culture. I hold my grandmother. Her fragile body. I never want to let go.

JEAN   I get on a plane, I'm going home. I'm leaving
                          home.

                          She picks up her suitcase.

                          *The sound of an airplane is heard as the lights
                          fade.*

Napoleon of the Nile

George Bwanika Seremba

George Bwanika Seremba was born in Kampala, Uganda. He started writing and acting at Makerere University, but it was during his years of exile in Kenya that he began to come into his own as an artist. Kenyan audiences remember him for his production of Athol Fugards's "Bloodknot". Since moving to Canada, he has appeared in numerous productions, including "Our Country's Good" at Alberta Theatre Projects, "Separate Development" at Great Canadian Theatre Company in Ottawa, "Majangwa" at the Manitoba Theatre Centre Warehouse, and "Master Harold and the Boys" at the Centaur Theatre, Montreal. He also starred in the 1990 feature film, "The Midday Sun", and has appeared in numerous television series. He recently played Mr. M in his fourth Fugard play, "My Children, My Africa!" His own plays include "Napoleon of the Nile and "Come Good Rain" , about his exile from and return to Uganda and his harrowing, near-death experiences under the cruel regime there.

Napoleon of the Nile

George Bwanika Seremba

The story of three individuals who are part of an exodus from the Sudan: Napoleon, a boy of 13 who leaves his family and home town and joins up with Mama Aleur, a woman of great resources, and Old Man, whose wisdom and knowledge help them through their journey. Napoleon eventually promises Old Man that he will tell the story of their crossing of the Nile.

The three characters hold imaginary oars.

OLD MAN	(*soon after the journey begins, turns to ALUER*) We need a coin.
ALEUR	What, the blanket wasn't enough?
OLD MAN	This is not a fee, it's a toll.
ALUER	You of all people, soliciting alms for the government.
OLD MAN	(*reverential*) To disabuse the mighty Nile. So we may fare forward.
ALUER	Fare forward...you make it sound like we are dead meat.
	OLD MAN sighs. ALUER hands him a coin; OLD MAN closes his eyes, and mumbles an inaudible prayer.
ALUER	Does that mean we shall sail in peace?

OLD MAN

Even if we don't, we've done our best. Left no stone unturned to placate the Tetrarch of all rivers.

NAPOLEON

Why placate when we've done nothing to provoke the river?

ALUER

Tell him Old One. Tell him. (*laughing*) Is it too long a story. We have twelve full hours (*taunting him as he takes his time*) You know what they say...

OLD MAN

The proud elder that boasts of hoarding a granary of proverbs from the young ones, simply happens to be masquerading ignorance.

> *His audience of two are all ears. There is a slow fade but the lights don't go to black. The drums start; it's a hypnotizing, almost timeless timbre that evokes and speaks of extinction and survival. The actors are frozen in this paradoxical tableau. He steps out of his — through a combination of light and colour. He appears to be walking on water that will gradually change to crimson.*

OLD MAN

In the beginning, the mighty Nile was a peaceful river. Peaceful as in Mother Nature and the periodical brutality and unpredictability of ecological affirmation and renewal. That was a long time ago. Long before the genesis of the SPCA, the environmentalists and all.

Then the British came and defaced the face of the sacred falls...time passed, and they left it swallowed and strangled in its wake. They'd already introduced the Nile Perch which wreaked havoc on the time honoured Tilapia.

Time passed and leaders came and went.

I will not dwell on what other people have seen and chronicled better than I ever would, about the post-independence era. The Union Jack did come down and we nurtured and bred a savage race that grew taller than life itself. Turned the lake and the Nile

into floating cemeteries for all that refused to keep
silent in the face of oppression. Others needed not
say anything. Tribe and creed alone were enough to
condemn them to untimely and brutal deaths. Still,
the Nile flowed unabated, and restrained itself from
any retribution. Hence the toll to thank it for not
flooding us all in its anguish and in the face of the
busloads of innocent lives that were flooded into
the disaffected river.

It did restrain itself indeed and what a magnanimous
act of restraint it was my friends: the adjoining
rivers and lakes, the spirits of the dead themselves
got together once in a while, still urging the Nile
to teach the continent to flood its banks, and strike
a mortal blow. Even as I speak I can't help but
shudder to think that if they ever get its ear on a
bad day, the Zambezi, the Umpopo, the Niger, the
Congo, even the little Athi River and the Sezibwa
have already vowed and promised to join hands and
teach the Continent to take care of itself and all the
children of Mother Africa.

We may not live to see that day though. There is a
new race of leaders that could split the vote of those
living under the cradle of the Nile. In fact, rumour
has it that some spirits have been sighted in places,
having the occasional wine and dancing along the
banks at the witching hour. Indeed, I would not be
surprised if they've asked the tetrarch of the
continent to do something about a new affliction.
An affliction so deadly that it claims far more lives
than all those that once clogged the arteries of the
Nile and threatened it to change its course.

> *Silence, back to canoe. They paddle away for
> awhile.*

ALUER

When is the last time you visited the source?

OLD MAN

Nineteen seventy three. Two years after Idi Amin
came to power. Avoided even a glimpse of it
whenever I drove along the bridge to visit with my
friend at the Ministry of Labour Office in Jinja. He

actually worked for the Workmen's Compensation Board, which sounds like a bit of an oxymoronic term if you ask me, for a government whose only stock in trade was the decimation of its citizens.

ALUER   I'm told that some people became allergic to fish.

OLD MAN   It was hard. You never knew what to find whenever you cut the fish open. My friend once found a brand new Timex watch ticking away in the gills of a Tilapia. Others fainted after finding people's thumbs, toes and nails.

NAPOLEON   Oh God, that makes famine sound like a blessing. No wonder you stopped your visits.

OLD MAN   To tell you the truth, I continued. Only in the mind though. Once a week at least.

ALUER   On Sundays.

OLD MAN   It had become like telling the beads of the rosary. I stopped that too.

NAPOLEON   You're talking ill of the rosary.

OLD MAN   Far from it. Far be it for me to condemn or judge anyone else's belief. Its a matter of choice. (*slight pause*) I escorted my friend on a trip to Lake Kyoga. We used a government Land Rover all the way up to Namasagali on the shores of Lake Kyoga. We drove back to Kampala. The car was full to the brim. He told me he was about to open a spare parts business, on the side, to combat the hard economic times...A few days later his picture appeared in the paper; naked and chained, kissing the President for Life's feet, accused of high treason and using a government vehicle to ferry guns. He faced a firing squad in full view of the public at the Queen Elizabeth Clock Tower.

ALUER   (*to herself*) You sometimes can't help but wonder if this is worth it after all. (*quiet and angry*) Was that around the same time the Archbishop was murdered?

OLD MAN   Yes. How did you know that?

ALUER   It's the nuns. I was still in the convent at the time.
                 We held an all night vigil at Precious Blood.

OLD MAN   ...YY OKOT, John Olobo, MZEE
                 ORYEMA...God bless their precious souls.

ALUER   They must have dumped their corpses in the
                 floating cemeteries...

OLD MAN   Yes, they sent the sand-laden coffins home to their
                 loved ones on condition they promised not to open
                 them.

NAPOLEON   I'm glad to have known you Old One. I feel very
                 privileged.

OLD MAN   So am I, my dear. I hope you don't live to regret it.

NAPOLEON   Was your friend a poet by any chance?

OLD MAN   No. The poets and playwrights had picked up the
                 guns long before that. He was just another man
                 with a conscience. Didn't have much of a choice.
                 Any whiff of suspicion of your tribe alone, were
                 enough to condemn you. They all wrote their
                 poetry in a baptism of blood.

ALUER   Let's hope they are all dancing away. Warding the
                 evil spirits off the mercurial river so we may all
                 fare forward and have safe passage.

OLD MAN   I have a little confession to make, some of our own
                 country men worked for the atrocious regimes
                 involved.

                          *The mosquitoes have now set in. NAPOLEON
                          is busy fighting them, visibly upset. Nobody
                          seems to notice.*

NAPOLEON   I suppose that means we can't go to Uganda then.

ALUER   (*light heartedly*) Maybe not, Napoleon.

OLD MAN Who knows? There is a tendency to forgive, even forget too soon. As the saying goes...a leopard kills but so does kindness. Once you forgive anyone who's committed a crime against humanity who's to say he won't strike again should he get a chance to get back into power.

NAPOLEON We still can go to Uganda.

OLD MAN We haven't even got across the Nile yet. Then there is one more river to cross; the Akobo, it's right by the border.

ALUER If you want to go to Uganda you would have to take a different direction.

NAPOLEON When shall we get to Ethiopia then?

OLD MAN Another two months.

NAPOLEON Two months?

OLD MAN Only two months.

NAPOLEON How long have we been walking?

OLD MAN Six months. Once we cross we'll take a little vacation. We need a week to rest and wait for all the others and then it's six weeks through Duk Fadiet and beyond. That's the land of the Dinka's. The army and the militia line the entire route. The terrain itself is hostile. Sand most of the way. The fountains hard to come by. You can walk for days without seeing a single tree. During the day you are an open target and at night you have the ambushes to contend with.

ALUER You shouldn't worry about it, Napoleon. By then we'll be so hunted, penned and decimated that we shall be turned into animals. Then the Society for the Prevention of Cruelty to Animals and the environment will cry out for us to God and the world for turning a deaf ear to our solitary voices in the wilderness.

Silence. OLD MAN knows where this argument is coming from and where it could lead.

NAPOLEON   Are there no people and organizations to cry out against inhumanity to fellow human beings?

OLD MAN   Plenty and they are fighting for us and lots of other human beings like us, all over the world.

NAPOLEON continues to fight the mosquitoes.

ALUER   They haven't helped me.

OLD MAN   You are being absurd.

ALUER   What's more absurd to care for animals and the environment or people whose plight has become worse than the animals?

NAPOLEON   I for one would pay attention to animals and mankind. We all need each other.

OLD MAN   Leave Mama Aluer alone, Napoleon. She just doesn't like animals.

ALUER   (*furious*) I love animals.

OLD MAN   You do?

ALUER   Of course I do.

NAPOLEON is frustrated. Woe upon any mosquitoes that land in his vicinity. He fidgets with his oar as if to separate the two adults pitted against each other.

***

Child

Yvette Nolan

Yvette Nolan is a playwright, director, performer and popular
theatre facilitator born in Prince Albert, Saskatchewan to an
Algonquin mother and an Irish immigrant father. She lives in
Winnipeg where she has worked in virtually every capacity in
theatre, from administrator to archvist to actor. She first
emerged as a playwright in 1990 with her critically and
popularly acclaimed play, "Blade:

Child

Yvette Nolan

*Two young women, Monica and Monique. Monica is native,
Monique white. Monica sits on the floor like a child, Monique
stands apart from her. They are not aware of each other, but their
stories take up from each other effortlessly, as if they were.*

MONICA

When I was very young, just a toddler, my family
broke up. There were all kinds of problems within
the family, there was alcohol abuse, and other
substance abuse, and oh all kinds of abuse. So my
family broke up. My mother stayed on the rez with
my other siblings, but I was very young and my
grandparents took me to live with them in the city.

MONIQUE

But the grandparents of this little girl were very
aware of the effects of disassociation, of
disenfranchisement of their people and they didn't
want to propogate this in any way, so they were
careful to develop the bond between the little girl
and her family on the reserve. And so they prepared
the little girl — Monica her name was, like my
name, Monique, but different — to go back to the
reserve and visit with her family.

MONICA

I remember they showed me pictures of the people I
was going to see on the rez, "This is your uncle
Harry, and here's your brother Max, and your
brother Peter, yes, that's right, that's Mama" and
they seemed excited about this trip so I guess I
thought I was excited too. "You'll have a good
time, Monique," my grandmother kept saying. She

sometimes called me Monique, the French way,
especially when it was a treat she was talking
about, like "Do you want an ice cream, Monique?"
or "Who wants to go to the zoo? Monique does?"
Like that. So off we went to the rez. It was winter I
remember, cold, raw, wicked.

MONIQUE   When I heard this story, it was my friend Irene who
told me, and I think the horror of it was just
destroying her, she's aboriginal too, and she really
had to tell someone, because I think it was
poisoning her, but when she was telling me, I
jumped in and said "Is the child dead?" because I
couldn't stand waiting to see where the story was
going, what this thing was that was eating up Irene
and I thought that that would be the worst thing
that could happen. And she said "no"...

MONICA   So we went to the rez that weekend and saw my
family, my mother, my uncles, my brothers.
And—

MONIQUE   And—

MONICA   And.

MONIQUE   And the brother of this child — raped her.

MONICA   He raped me.

MONIQUE   Raped her.

MONICA   Raped me.

MONIQUE   She was four years old.

MONICA   Four years old.

MONIQUE   Only four.

MONICA   Only four.

Long pause.

MONIQUE   My heart began to break then, but it didn't break all
                 at once, it took all day and all night, and late that
                 night I found myself crying for that child, and I
                 didn't think I could stop, I didn't want to stop, I
                 wanted to cry away the hurt, to cry until I was
                 exhausted.

MONICA   Only four.

MONIQUE   She was only four for God's sake!

MONICA   And suddenly the world was a terrible, horrifying,
                 menacing place and suddenly I was afraid, afraid that
                 I would never be safe again, afraid that I would be
                 hurt by someone else I loved, afraid that I was too
                 much trouble and my grandparents were going to
                 send me away from them, and I began to search
                 around in myself for ways to pretend that I wasn't
                 there, so that no one would notice me and think to
                 send me away. I decided to be very, very quiet, and I
                 wrapped myself in blackness, the blackness that I
                 thought would protect me.

MONIQUE   I was so distraught, I couldn't stop thinking about
                 this, and I knew it happened all the time, but I just
                 felt so connected to this child to this poor little girl
                 and that night I lay in bed and I couldn't sleep and I
                 tried to pray for her, to save her from scarring, you
                 know, to make her feel that she was still valuable
                 that she wasn't damaged in any way.

MONICA   and night after night, for weeks after the visit, I
                 would lie there so wrapped in fear and terror and
                 hurt, just this huge hurt

MONIQUE   and I thought, will God intervene? Why would he if
                 he let it happen in the first place, and I thought if
                 only I could send myself out, if only I could go to
                 comfort that child and I concentrated very hard, and
                 I sent myself out into the air, out of my room and
                 into the night, and it was so cold, but I kept going

                         Through this next section, the two pools of
                         lights brighten and become one.

MONICA   and one night, lying there wrapped in my fear,
                      suffocating with terror I suddenly felt this warmth,
                      this heat pouring into me and it was light, like, not
                      lighting up my room, my little bed and my new
                      teddy bear that I'd been given like some prize for
                      getting through it, but a light inside me, in my
                      head — in my all and suddenly I felt that I was
                      loved and I was wanted and that this terrible hurt
                      that I felt, that it was a mistake somehow, and it
                      couldn't be taken away but it didn't have to take up
                      all of inside me because this warm feeling, this
                      light was filling me up, pushing out the blackness,
                      pushing out the hurt, or at least keeping it
                      cowering back in a tiny little corner of my all, and
                      I knew that someone cared for me now and would
                      care for me later

                              During this section, MONIQUE actually sees
                              MONICA, almost touches her.

MONIQUE   and you know, for a moment there I almost felt
                      like I could see that little girl there in that room
                      and I tried so hard to say to her, it's all right
                      sweetheart, it's all right, you are really all right,
                      you are, but I just couldn't make the words come
                      out and I just couldn't keep the picture in my head
                      and I don't know if she got my message

MONICA   and then the warmth drained away and the light died
                      down and that feeling subsided, but it didn't go
                      away completely, it stayed, a tiny little flickering
                      light, a spark even, that glowed in me, in my all,
                      and it glows in me still. And sometimes it burns
                      brightly like a lighter at a rock concert, and
                      sometimes it barely sparks, but I tend it, you
                      know, I shelter it and I feed it so it is always there
                      and will always be there

MONIQUE   oh I wished there was some way I could help that
                      little girl, and I wished for her many times over the
                      years, and I wished that somehow my wishes would
                      protect her, and that night I would have given
                      anything to be able to comfort her in some way
                      because the pain I felt for her was so great.

MONICA   I have a little girl now — huh! Funny, eh? I called her Helen, and I try to teach this to her, about this spark that burns so brightly in each of us, and how important it is that we care for that spark and not let it be swallowed up by the blackness.

***

Kyotopolis

Daniel David Moses

Daniel David Moses is a Delaware from the Six Nations of the Grand River who lives in Toronto, writing full time and working with both Native and cross cultural arts organisations. His plays include "The Moon and the Dead Princess" (winner of the duMaurier One-Act Playwriting Competition), "Almighty Voice and His Wife", "Big Buck City", "Belle Fille de L'Aurore", "The Dreaming Beauty" (First Prize, National Playwriting Competition, One-Act Category), and "Coyote City".

Kyotopolis

Daniel David Moses

*Who was that woman we saw riding the space shuttle
last night, riding it right into orbit — and the obituaries? An
Indian Princess? A New Age Shamaness? Or just little Babe
Fisher? Even her family isn't sure anymore. A darkly comic
fantasia about the ways we communicate and the future of Native
identity in The Global Village. Ricky Raccoon is just one of the
many characters she encounters.*

> *RICKY falls out of a mad dancing spin. A
> monitor on-stage fills with the night city. A
> ray of moon light comes up slowly on
> RICKY.*

No news, that's good news, right? Right? I keep my mouth shut and you
can't get a hold on me. You don't know what to think, what to feel. You
can't get me. That's what you want to do, that's what you're here for. You
want to know how he feels. How how how the famous Indian host of the
long-running Tommy Hawk and the Little Fuckers feels now now now
that the little people are dead. Tommy's oh so delicious, you want to eat
him up, just like you did with them little folks. But it's too late for that,
cuz he was one of them little buggers too, ya, Tommy Hawk, he's gone
like a fart, gone west, passed over, up in smoke. And there's nobody in
here but us Raccoons. And you don't want to know how how how we feel
now, do you? You don't want to know what we think, do you? We aren't
Indian enough, are we? Or are we like too Indian for you to chew? Are
you hungry enough now finally to eat anything? Are you? Are you? Well
chew on this. Sorry if it's kind of wooden. It's not news but it's good.
The Raccoon was alone in the city. Don't know why. Let's say he
thought the lights was pretty. Let's say his momma got run over by some
drunk. Let's say his brother with the bright dark eyes one day did a dance
at the end of a rope. Was it an Indian dance? A fairy dance? Something
like that. Ya, the Raccoon was alone and hungry, he would have got
stoned if he'd had the money. He would maybe even have tried the dance

himself if he'd had the guts. Fairies can't grant themselves wishes, ay?
Hey let's come right out and say the Raccoon then wanted to be dead. But
then this Indian girl, this Indian girl with bright dark eyes said, 'Hey little
brother, have you seen my sister?' And he thought he had.

> *The night city image on the monitor cross*
> *fades to the petroglyphs.*

What do you think about babies with bright dark eyes? Are you in favour
of them? I am. I'd do anything to look after them. You can't let the
cannibals get at them. Hey that's what it's like in the big town. You got
to look after your own. Hey I'd even become an Uncle Tomahawk. Would
you like a cigar?

> *The monitor cuts to a silent image of FRED*
> *FACE reporting and then to another of a*
> *missile being launched.*

It's so nice to have a niece around the house. Let's say the Raccoon took
the baby in. It was a hole under an old theatre where the fairies boogied in
their rings. Where the fairies went to get bombed. And those who knew
the Babe was down there were called Darling, Dear, Bitch and Mary, fairy
godmothers all.

> *The monitor shows a silent image of a distant,*
> *star-bright missile hitting the shuttle and*
> *blowing it apart in a flare of light.*

And they all conspired to take care of her and give her presents and
blessings. And you know she slept in a trunk full of boas and bear skin
— bare skin? — for years. No wonder she became a star! No wonder she
stole our hearts. No wonder she disappeared!

> *The monitor image whites out and then the*
> *face of MARY, another character, appears in an*
> *extreme close up, pressed against the glass, but*
> *then quickly the monitor sparks and goes dead*
> *as the spot on RICKY goes out. The*
> *petroglyphs flare and then fade to black.*

***

One Ocean

Betty Quan

Betty Quan was born in Vancouver and has been based in Toronto since 1986. A freelance editor and writer, her work encompasses radio and stage adaptations and script consultation / story editing. She has just served a residency at the Canadian Film Centre and is currently consulting on a feature film script as well as developing her own two-hour teleplay. Upcoming work for stage includes an adaptation of Joy Kogawa's book, *Naomi's Road*, for Young People's Theatre 1996 school touring programme, and the libretto for a new opera, "Iron Road", to be produced in 1997 by Tapestry Music Theatre.

One Ocean

Betty Quan

Using the Chinese myth of the Jingwei bird, a daughter tries to bridge the physical and emotional gulf with her father in this memory play about the ideas of immigration and subsequent separation of families.

This play aired on CBC "Morningside", radio drama program on December 20, 1994.

Scene 1: Narration. Inside memory.
Music: establish theme, continue under.

DAUGHTER (older) A long time ago. It was my favourite. A story. No, our story. Just a Chinese folktale. Yes. About the Jingwei bird and why she is always dropping sticks and stones in the ocean. When I was small, I used to pretend I was that little bird. I would soar through our communal courtyard with arms for wings. That was when we were still allowed to enjoy our stories, to tell our stories, before, before...*Bah-bah.* Father. Do you remember like I do? Tell me about the Jingwei. Yes, like you used to do when I was small. You told me that story when I left Hong Kong for Canada. Do you remember? I was sad. We were both sad. Like a bird in your hand I was until you set me free across the sky, across the ocean. Such a long time ago, yet so close I can still see it unfolding before me. Father? Tell me a story. Like you used to do. (*as if repeating what she hears in memory*) "A long time ago." It seems like yesterday. A long time ago. But

that is how we begin our stories, isn't it? We begin
with "a long time ago."

Scene 2: Folktale Remembered.

FATHER   A long time ago there was an emperor who had a
                  young daughter. They loved each other very much.
                  But although his powers could touch all corners of
                  the land, the emperor could see only as far as the
                  shoreline that divided his kingdom with the sea.

DAUGHTER   Beyond that shoreline, his vision was limited, like
                  a kite held high in a strong breeze — he could see
                  the shape, but not the colours.

                  Music ends. Sound effects: birds, breeze,
                  ocean, continue under:

DAUGHTER   Father, look at the waves, so tall they must be
                  hiding something behind them. I will take my boat
                  for a ride.

FATHER   (*as Emperor*) Not so far, not so far.

DAUGHTER   (*as Jingwei*) Don't worry, Father. I'll be careful.

FATHER   (*as Emperor*) Why don't you wait a while? I'll join
                  you. We can journey to the horizon together, where
                  the sea meets the sun.

DAUGHTER   (*as Jingwei*) When? When can we do this?
                  (*laughing*) You're always promising such things,
                  Father! You're too busy as Emperor. I'll go out on
                  my own first. On my own adventure. Then, I'll
                  show you what I've seen.

FATHER   (*as Emperor, laughing*) When?

DAUGHTER   (*as Jingwei*) What does that matter? We have all the
                  time in the world.

DAUGHTER (older) The sun was warm upon the little girl's face—

FATHER — and the salty breeze off the water tempted her to travel farther and farther. To see what hid behind the tall waves of the sea.

DAUGHTER (older) Far far far away she went, when suddenly—

Sound effects: thunder and rainstorm.

FATHER (*as Sea God*) Who dares come this far upon the ocean of my reign?

DAUGHTER (older) The Sea God's bad temper came upon the little girl.

Sound effects: Jingwei screams as the waves engulf her.

FATHER The water became a blanket that covered her. And the little girl died.

Sound effects: all suddenly end.

DAUGHTER (older) Died? I don't remember her dying. Is that right? I thought the water changed her into a bird. Like magic.

FATHER I would tell you that when you were small. When you didn't understand death.

DAUGHTER (older) Like I do now.

FATHER It is only a story. (*continues*) The little girl's soul became a small bird called Jingwei.

Music begins.

DAUGHTER (older) Father, I died that day you sent me away.

FATHER No, child, you were reborn. Now, continue the story.

DAUGHTER

Angry was the spirit in that bird, angry at the sea it was for taking her away from her beloved father. And every day the Jingwei would carry in her beak stones and twigs from the mountains of the east and flying west ahead drop her small stones and twigs into the sea. And the Sea God finally noticed what Jingwei was trying to do.

Music ends. Sound effects: ocean. Close: the wings of a bird in motion.

FATHER

(*as Sea God, laughing*) Silly creature, my sea is wider and deeper than your limited imagination. You can never fill me up in a million years.

DAUGHTER

(*as Jingwei*) But I can. Every day for a million years I will do this. Every day until one day. Until one day...(*begin fade down*) Until one day...Until one day...

FATHER

And the small bird flew back to land —

FATHER & DAUGHTER (older)

— only to return with another small stone or twig to drop into the sea.

DAUGHTER (older)

And Jingwei said: "One day, there will be a bridge between me and my father. One day, even if it takes a million years to build it." (*she no longer speaks as the Jingwei*) Soon, father. I will see you again. Soon.

Sound effects: fade down.

Scene 3. Airport.

Sound effects: airplane's acceleration and ascent. Fades into airport interior: Chinese public address system etc. Close: a swallow singing

FATHER

Yes, yes, sing a goodbye song to my daughter. Here's a sunflower seed.

DAUGHTER	I don't think pets are allowed here.
FATHER	This is not just a pet, eh my little friend? Now keep your bag in full sight. Many pickpockets. There is more freedom here in Hong Kong but that doesn't mean there is less danger. Here's your ticket. Show it to that man over there. Where's your passport?
DAUGHTER	I don't want to go to Vancouver, father. Why me?
FATHER	Your big brother has a family now. You will go first, then settle down. Then we can join you.
DAUGHTER	When?
FATHER	Soon. Soon. Look at us now. We used to have a fine house and good food to eat. First the Japanese and the war, now Mao. Remember, just a few years ago, Mao decided China must have its Great Leap Forward? And the country went two steps forward and five steps back?

Scene 4: Narration. Inside Memory. Music fades under:

DAUGHTER (older) Mosquitos, flies, rats, and sparrows: Mao called these the "four pests." 1958: it was the year I turned sixteen. (*bitter laugh*) Do you remember? Mao believed grain production was down because the sparrows were feeding on the backs of the people. Families were armed with pots and pans. We were to scare the sparrows out of the trees so they would eventually drop dead from exhaustion. 600 million of us, running under trees, in the countryside, in the cities, making enough noise to waken the dead. Yes, the sparrows ate the grain, but they also ate the insects. Without the sparrows, no one could control the insects. The sky would rain the corpses of little birds to join the corpses of 300 million people, dead of starvation.

Scene 5: Airport. Sound effects: airport interior. Close: the swallow singing

FATHER   You know how lucky we were to get out of China?

DAUGHTER   I know.

FATHER   How can we Chinese have luck when we are killing birds!? This is why it is good we are here now. No more death. No more hunger. No more sacrificing our own symbols of fortune and happiness. Maybe my good luck has returned right here in this cage. Maybe now we will all have good luck.

DAUGHTER   Maybe's, nothing but maybe's.

FATHER   You have a chance now, can't you see? To start a new life in a new place.

DAUGHTER   Let me finish school first.

FATHER   (*joking*) Maybe, you'll find a rich Canadian and marry him.

DAUGHTER   I'm 18 years old; I don't need a husband. I can try to find a job here, in Hong Kong.

FATHER   Just a temporary thing, you'll see. Your mother, your brother, me. We'll be a family again. We're relying on you. Work hard. Stay out of trouble. Be a citizen your new country can be proud of. When you're settled, you'll sponsor us to come. We'll join you later.

DAUGHTER   Please don't make me go, father.

FATHER   Who is the parent here? Who makes the decision?

DAUGHTER   Please, father, don't make me go all alone.

FATHER   Look, my Jingwei. Yes, you have always been like a little bird to me. If I could, I would always try to protect you, away from bad things. But this — this — is a good thing.

DAUGHTER	I don't want to go!
FATHER	Believe me, it's for the best. You'll like it in Canada.
DAUGHTER	Don't you want me to stay here, with you?
FATHER	It doesn't matter what I want. It's what I want for you.
FEMALE	(*over sound system, filtered*)Last boarding call for Flight 973 departing for Vancouver, Canada.

The announcer repeats this in Cantonese.

DAUGHTER	I've never been in a plane before, Father. Have you?
FATHER	No. Not yet. But in time, no?
DAUGHTER	Yes, in time.

Scene 6: Airfield. Sound effects: airport exterior. Plane accelerating and ascending. Closer: the swallow's song.

FATHER   Goodybe! (*to himself*) Goodbye.

Sound effects: Swallow singing.

FATHER   What's that? What are you singing about?

                *Sound effects: swallow singing. Metal clink of
                the cage being opened.*

FATHER   Come on, there. No, it's not a trick. Out. Yes. Fly,
                go on, fly. Fly.

                *Sound effects: Close: the acceleration of a
                bird's wings, heard under:*

FATHER   Build a bridge between me and my daughter. Make
                our ocean one.

                *Scene 7: Narration - Inside Memory. Music:
                begins and continues under:*

DAUGHTER (older) You broke your promise. You never came. You let
                me leave you behind. I waited for you, Father. For
                the family. A long time ago. Where are you? Are
                you here, with me? Did you follow on the shadow
                of the airplane's wings? (*voice begins to break*) Did
                I fly away like a kite in the breeze? So high up you
                can see the shape, but not the colours? Can you see
                me? I'm so far away but all you have to do is pull
                me home. Father. Father. When I finish building a
                bridge, will you cross it? Even if the stones are
                loose, and the twigs are breaking. Will you cross
                it? Father? (*beat*) *Bah-bah?* How big is the ocean?

                *Music ends. Sound effects: exterior: airfield.
                Plane's acceleration and ascent crosses into that
                of birds in flight, their wings in motion. Fade
                into ocean, water lapping on a beach. Up and
                out.*

                              ***

Encore

Dirk McLean

Dirk McLean was born in Trinidad in 1956 and moved to Canada at the age of 13. He later graduated from The Royal Conservatory of Music in Speech and Drama. He has written for the stage, screen and radio, and has completed the manuscript of "The House on Hermitage Road", an autobiographical novel about his childhood in Trinidad. This was also the basis for a 5-part CBC Radio play on Morningside Drama in 1991. He is also an actor of stage and screen. He serves on the advisory board of Cahoots Theatre Projects. His other plays include "Shall We Call a Teacher?", and "The Real McCoy" (co-writer).

Encore

Dirk McLean

*Loners Adriel, and Sally, both in their late 20's, claim
to have sworn off relationships, yet either of them
would be willing to re-open their hearts if the right
person were to come along — especially with an
invisible spiritual guide ready to nudge them.*

*They have both been invited to a Halloween party by
mutual friends, Desmond and Carmen, but are bored
there. This is their first encounter.*

	Act One, Scene Three. Lights come up on DESMOND and CARMEN's backyard. A middle-class residence. It is a clear area; except for a few white chairs scattered in various positions. Coloured balloons are hung across the yard. Latin American music is heard coming from one side. We see ADRIEL dancing with a chair. After a moment SALLY enters, unseen by ADRIEL, and observes him as she sips her soda and lemon. Both are wearing colourful costumes. African. Tribal. Ancient. But allowing free movement. Finally, SALLY speaks as the music fades.
SALLY	Wouldn't you rather be dancing with someone?
	ADRIEL stops in his tracks. HE looks behind him and sees SALLY; puts down the chair.
ADRIEL	They're all married, and jealous.
SALLY	I'm not. Married or jealous.

ADRIEL   Did Carmen send you here?

SALLY   Pardon?

ADRIEL   It's nothing.

SALLY   I have a mind of my own. I don't need this.

                    SALLY turns to leave.

ADRIEL   I'm sorry. She's always trying to...

                    SALLY begins to walk away.

ADRIEL   I'm entitled to a second chance at...talking with
                    you...l'd like to talk

SALLY   Why?

ADRIEL   We have mutual friends.

SALLY   (*facing ADRIEL*) I came out here looking for you
                    'cause I thought you'd be the most interesting man
                    at this party.

ADRIEL   And I've disappointed you.

SALLY   Carmen said you were...she said you were worth
                    talking to. She talked about you a lot. (*pause*)
                    Well, don't you want to know what she said?

ADRIEL   No.

SALLY   You're pretty self-assured, eh?

ADRIEL   Yes.

SALLY   Honest too. I like that.

ADRIEL   Would you like to sit down?

SALLY   I like your paintings.

ADRIEL	You know my work?
SALLY	Not all of it. Just the two pieces in the living-room. Carmen and I discussed them. Size. Texture. Emotion. Colour. Vibes. You used the same woman for both paintings. Are you one of those artists who uses the same model until she dies?
ADRIEL	(*laughing*) I'm no Dally, if that's your reference. But I love his work. (*beat*) It's Carmen, anyway.
SALLY	Nooooooo.
ADRIEL	Would I lie to you?
SALLY	I don't know. (*beat*) They don't look like her. Why didn't she tell me?
ADRIEL	She enjoys mystery. As you probably know, Carmen loves to siesta.
SALLY	Yes.
ADRIEL	(*moving to close the gap a little*) One afternoon, Desmond invited me over to watch her.
SALLY	I didn't think they were that kind of couple.
ADRIEL	(*laughing*) I'd never thought of that.
SALLY	I would.
ADRIEL	He'd always wanted me to paint her, but she hates posing. The interesting thing was that she leaves her body when she sleeps, and the face transforms.
SALLY	Oh, my!
ADRIEL	That's what Desmond wanted me to capture. He wanted a whole series. Carmen stopped us after the second one.
SALLY	Couldn't you have continued sneaking into their bedroom and...

ADRIEL	I observe people, I'm not a voyeur.
SALLY	If I were to do something daring like take off my clothes, I bet you wouldn't turn away.
ADRIEL	Do you always talk this way to strangers?
SALLY	Carmen said you were kinda serious. I'm taking liberties. I wanted to see how serious a man who paints with so much sensuality could be. I didn't think I'd find you dancing with a chair.
ADRIEL	How long did you watch?
SALLY	Long enough to tell that a) You're a good dancer. b) You're starving for company. And c) I can understand your need to get away from them in there. Will you dance with me?
ADRIEL	You're so forward.
SALLY	You pretend to be shy.
ADRIEL	I am.
SALLY	You don't have to be shy with me.
ADRIEL	Don't need a second invitation, then.

ADRIEL strikes a dance pose.

SALLY	I never issue second invitations.

SALLY strikes a dance pose opposite ADRIEL, who looks at her for a moment. He begins to dance, moving towards SALLY as the music swells. Then SALLY joins him. They never touch. But it's very sensual, verging on erotic — yet never vulgar. There is an animal magnetism between them, and it's as though they've done this before together. The dance should be more organic than polished. About three minutes; amongst the chairs. The music ends. They stand still looking at each

other. Finally, as the music continues,
distantly, SALLY moves away, coming
downstage centre, and looks out.

SALLY	The moon.
ADRIEL	Ummm? Sorry.
SALLY	I said the moon.
ADRIEL	(*joining SALLY*) It's, er, full.
SALLY	She's beautiful.
ADRIEL	Wouldn't you just die if it started to move.
SALLY	I'd think I was drunk. Do you suppose she's one of those false gods we're not supposed to worship?
ADRIEL	I dunno. You look gorgeous in this moonlight, whatever your name is.
SALLY	I knew it. A shy man would never dare speak to me like that. It's Sally.
ADRIEL	Adriel.
SALLY	I remember.
ADRIEL	You're the dressmaker.
SALLY	I'm a designer.
ADRIEL	Sorry.
SALLY	I designed and made Carmen's wedding dress. And I do much more.
ADRIEL	What's your line called?
SALLY	Miss Sally.
ADRIEL	Not Ms. ?

SALLY   Feminism is not just in a word.

ADRIEL   Most movements begin with a word.

SALLY   Name one.

ADRIEL   Da!

SALLY   Da? Irish word. Father. Fatherhood. Movement of
               Fathers?

ADRIEL   No, no no, you are too literary. It is much simpler
               than that. And quite well-known, too.

SALLY   Are you trying to make me look stupid?

ADRIEL   I don't know you well enough to attempt such a
               conquest.

SALLY   Is it a Black movement?

ADRIEL   It transcends colour.

SALLY   I'm getting too impatient to continue with your
               charade.

ADRIEL   Here it is: (*opening notes of the First Movement of
               Beethoven's Fifth Symphony*) DA DA DA,
               DAAAAAAAH!

               SALLY laughs. Both laugh.

SALLY   And here I thought you were politically-inclined.

ADRIEL   I am. My political issue, and sub-issues, stem from
               the word LOVE. It's a movement. It's definitely a
               movement. It's in all of my work. I paint people
               kissing, embracing, touching. In one of my
               paintings a woman is touching her face. Her eyes
               are closed. And you know what she's thinking. I've
               refused to sell it on several occasions. It's a sort of
               yardstick for some of my other work. In another
               painting you see a man and a woman holding hands
               walking towards you. I show only a portion of

their bodies, the hands are the main focal point. And beyond the hands in the background, is a city. Ice-cold. Greys. Muddy purple. Black. They are leaving that city behind. I don't show what they're going towards. You can well imagine. My 1990's painting. Before you say anything, it's not altogether bleak, for they have the strength and the courage to leave. And they are not fleeing in horror as you might expect. If we get to know each other, I will show you. If not, I have an exhibition next month, God willing.

SALLY   It all looks bleak, anyway.

ADRIEL   I don't believe that. Some changes. Some belt-tightening. I still intend to wake up smiling.

SALLY   You're serious.

ADRIEL   Always.

SALLY   I'm not in the mood for that, tonight. The people in the painting, though, what are they wearing?

ADRIEL   (*laughing*) Ah, I will keep you in suspense. I know now that you will see that painting. I'm glad I came to this party.

SALLY   Yeah...me, too. A gathering.

ADRIEL   A meeting. (*pause*) Do you ever leave your body?

SALLY   Why would I want to do that?

ADRIEL   When you sleep, I meant. Not everyone's aware that they do. But most people do.

SALLY   Do you?

ADRIEL   I think so.

SALLY   And what do you do then? Visit your friends? See the world?

ADRIEL   Probably.

SALLY   I really didn't expect a reply.

ADRIEL   I know. (*beat*) I think I help people.

SALLY   What? Like who?

ADRIEL   People who are sick. Or desperate. Or dying.

SALLY   All right. I'm liberal. I've come across a few of those articles, myself. But I've never ever met anyone making such confessions directly to me.

ADRIEL   Don't ask for proof. I have none.

SALLY   I believe that. Hey, all I'm gonna say on the subject is...I never leave my body.

                    Pause.

ADRIEL   I'm inclined to think people in the subway do.

SALLY   What?

ADRIEL   On buses and streetcars. It's like they're not really there. I'm sure they leave their bodies. Even in the elevators — people have their eyes fixed to the numbers, but they're not looking at the numbers. Nope, they're 'out there' somewhere. Especially crossing the street; folks run right into me and don't...

SALLY   Enough! Please. (*beat*) You know, I think I asked Carmen all the wrong questions about you. I should have asked about your mind.

ADRIEL   You don't have to be afraid of what you don't know, Sally.

SALLY   Right. I suppose you've conquered all your fears.

ADRIEL	No. I'm afraid to drive a car. I'm almost thirty years old, and I don't have a driver's licence. How about that?
SALLY	You're serious!
ADRIEL	Always.
SALLY	I can't think of my life without a car.

There is a pause. They look at the moon.

SALLY	Nice costume.
ADRIEL	Thanks. I like yours, too.
SALLY	I made it.

ADRIEL kisses SALLY's hand, briefly. She leans into it, but does not hold him. He lets go of her hand.

SALLY	Oooooooouh! There's a sudden chill. Do you always kiss strange women this soon?
ADRIEL	No. Only you. I'm not sure what made me do it.
SALLY	Don't apologize.
ADRIEL	I didn't.
SALLY	Must have been some little devil. (*pause*) There's a sadness I get from you. A deep sadness. Why?
ADRIEL	Don't know. It's always been there.
SALLY	(*moving away after an awkward moment*) I'm hungry. What do you say we split from here and find a nice restaurant.
ADRIEL	Do I make you nervous?
SALLY	No...no.

ADRIEL	What do you feel like eating?
SALLY	What? (*still thinking about the 'sadness'*)
ADRIEL	You heard me.
SALLY	What do you feel like eating?
ADRIEL	That's a strange question to ask a strange man.
SALLY	I wish you hadn't done that.
ADRIEL	Done what?
SALLY	Kissed me.
ADRIEL	You didn't like it?
SALLY	I did. It feels like rain. Let's drive around until we decide on something.
ADRIEL	Okay.
SALLY	(*as they begin to exit*) I hate driving in the rain.
ADRIEL	What make?
SALLY	Hundai. Red. You'll have to buckle up.

Lights fade.

***

Thy Creature Blues

H. Jay Bunyan

H. Jay Bunyan is a native of Guyana. A graduate of Ryerson Polytechnical Institute, he is now the Artistic Co-ordinator of Theatre in Exile. *Thy Creature Blues* is the ninth play he has written and produced. His other plays include *Prodigals in a Promised Land* and *Three Beats to the Bar*.

Thy Creature Blues

Hector Jay Bunyan

Dr. Jansen, a psychiatrist, is relating to a client the important role her son had played in her life and in the world he inhabited prior to his death.

Dr. Jansen

You know, Daniel, I used to teach at the National University in your country. One day, my son, Eugene, came to pick me up. He was a bit early, so he sat quietly at the back of my class. On the way home I was expecting to hear him say, "Myrna, you were excellent! Your class blew me away!" because I was superb. Nothing but silence from him. I thought, maybe he's had a rough day, even though I was pissed-off, because he knew what he thought of me and my work meant the world to me. I allowed him his mood for a while, then I asked him why he was so silent. He asked me not to say anything until we arrived where he was taking me. He said he felt I was ready to meet his friends. It turned out to be a church which provided hot meals and clothing for the needy.

What stood before me was the horror of destitution and the failure of my work to connect my students to this forgotten segment of society. I felt a wrenching sadness for the children among this group because, despite the cruelty of the streets where they made their home, theirs were the eyes of children everywhere: luminous and innocent and full of giggles and shy and eager to trust and anxious to please and if you should hug them, they would weep their sadness away. Gene said quite often a group of children would appear without one or two of their regular members. The children would blithely declare that the absent ones "have gone back home". That was their way of saying a comrade had died, more likely than not, murdered to rid the society of what some considered to be human garbage, and not a word of that execution would sully the pages of the newspaper, or even earn a fleeting mention on the radio or television. The media ensured that no messy detail would interrupt the soap opera of middle class existence. Yet in spite of the precariousness of those children's lives, they would display a rather carefree attitude that left Gene and the other volunteers quite perplexed. What they couldn't understand was that those children had learnt to befriend death, because it meant the end of disappointment and pain and the only secure home they would ever be able to call their own.

The emotional toll on the volunteers was severe. They were dropping out faster than they could be replaced. That's when the remaining volunteers decided they had to find a way to deal with their pain in a meaningful way...they needed to grieve the deaths of these children who had become so much a part of their lives, often much closer to them than their own relatives.

At Gene's suggestion, they would commence with grace before meals. At the head of the central table, a place was prepared for those friends who "have gone back home". A place-mat of velvet was decorated with gleaming cutlery and china of the finest vintage. Those who won't ever return were the first to be served.

Gene led the proceedings by invoking their names. At this roll-call of the dead, a hush fell upon the dining-hall:

"CheeChee...Cinderella...Rainbow...The Duchess...Prince and Princess Charming....Her Majesty...Doctor...The Professor"...each name acknowledged by a child's hand, rising slowly above the rows of heads, bowed in reverence, each hand displaying a memento from one of the deceased: a doll's leg...the wheel of a toy truck...a used toothbrush...a coil of electrical wire...a broken comb...a pair of baby's booties...the remains of a stethoscope...

"To you our friends, cradled in eternal sleep in the company of angels, we dedicate this meal to your memory" Then, in unison, a dining-hall of ragged and forgotten souls repeated the words, "Be present at our table Lord, Be here and everywhere adored, Thy creatures bless and grant that we may feast in paradise with thee, Amen."

Short pause.

And then something broke...something very delicate that each man, each woman, each child in that dining-hall had been carrying around for a long time, hidden away from each other, perhaps hidden from the self. Out of these broken souls rushed a river of grief that made them collapse into each other's embrace. For the duration of the meal, hardly a sound was heard; not even the sound of cutlery on plate which was so remarkable when you consider that these were almost five hundred hungry people! Such was the depth of their reverence! There in that dining-hall among the outcasts of society, my life was irrevocably changed. Here was a seventeen year-old engaging in healing the spirits of the wretched, giving them the power to die with dignity, while on the other side of the city, his mother, a trained psychiatrist, was pacifying the anguish of the middle class and training others to do the same; and, at the end of the day, I would retire to my home convinced that I had served life's deeper purpose. Here was a seventeen year-old who was not interested in recognition, not even among the group where he concentrated his energies. He felt that was obscene. Yet in his own quiet way, he was making life sing its song of praise for those who had heard only a song of sorrow. He was making a goddamn revolution!

Pause.

Less than two weeks later he was dead...snatched away by the secret-police...and what was his crime? My beautiful friend...my beautiful young lion...the best teacher I've ever had...another spiritual warrior...no more to come home to.

Pause.

And if your daughter should ever say to you one day, "Be honest with me dad, is there any point in carrying on?" Tell her that once there was a seventeen year-old who allowed himself to be touched by the cry of the wounded among us, and at least once a week, he gave them a reason to transcend their harsh reality; he gave them a reason to live with dignity in the immanence of death.

***

Someday

Drew Hayden Taylor

Drew Hayden Taylor is an Ojibway writer from the Curve
Lake First Nations in Central Ontario. In his past 33 years, he
has written television scripts for "The Beachcombers", "Street
Legal", and "North of Sixty". His plays include: "Toronto at
Dreamer's Rock" — 11 productions, winner of the Chalmers
Playwrighting Award for Best Play for Young Audiences -
1992; "Bootlegger Blues" — 4 productions, winner of the
Canadian Authors Association Literary Award for Drama;
"Someday" — 4 productions; and most recently "Girl Who
Loved Her Horses", and "The Baby Blues".

Also an experienced journalist, articles and commentaries by
Drew have appeared on CBC Radio, *Macleans* magazine, *This
Magazine*, *The Globe and Mail*, *The Toronto Star*, and *Books
in Canada* among others. He is currently working on two
movie projects and the sequel to "Someday", and has been the
Artistic Director of Native Earth Performing Arts, Toronto's
only professional Native theatre company.

Someday

Drew Hayden Taylor

*Years ago, on the Otter Lake Reserve, Anne Wabung's
daughter, Grace, was taken away by Children's Aid
workers when the girl was only a toddler. It is
Christmas, 35 years later, and Anne's yearning to see
her now-grown daughter, christened Janice, is stronger
than ever. When the family is reunited, including
Anne's other daughter, Barb, and her boyfriend Rodney,
the dreams of neither woman are fulfilled. ANNE has
also just won a lottery.*

> *In ANNE's house. ANNE enters, followed by
> RODNEY. She turns up the thermostat and
> puts the kettle on.*

ANNE   Tea, I need tea. Rodney?

RODNEY   Yes, please.

ANNE   All them reporters, cameras. I've never shaked so
many hands. *(holding up her hand)* It feels like five
pieces of spaghetti. You'd think Indians never won
anything before. Can you imagine the nerve of the
chief flagging us down this morning to try and
borrow some money? Twelve years ago when
Frank was a councillor and still alive I begged him
to talk to the chief about getting our peoples' kids
back from the Children's Aid Society, but Frank
just got mad. "Let sleeping dogs lie" was all he
said, rest his soul, and I said my Grace wasn't a
dog, she was my baby. "She's somebody else's
now. She's dead to us, Anne. Let her rest." Dead to

us. I went behind his back and spoke to the chief myself. Wouldn't do nothing, not a blessed thing. People on this reserve are still afraid of them.

RODNEY   Who?

ANNE   The C.A.S. I was storming their offices in downtown Toronto when you were still in diapers, boy. They'd had their screaming Indian women before but I took the cake. Wouldn't leave — I sat down and said I wasn't going to let up till I'd seen my own daughter's file.

RODNEY   What happened?

ANNE   They called the cops and threw me in their car. Real rough on me, too! Said I was "fixated." Find me a mother in my situation who isn't. Them people, they're no damn good. Cradle snatchers. That's the whole long and short of it, nothing more than common kidnappers!

RODNEY   But Anne, they got Indian case workers now. Hell, my aunt's been working with them for years.

ANNE   And I've had my suspicions about your Aunt Julia, Rodney. No offence.

RODNEY   Okay, but you take away the C A.S. and who is gonna look after the kids who are really getting hurt?

ANNE   Let our own people tell them who they should take, and where they should take them, and for how long. Don't let them come walking in cool as the breeze into our homes without so much as a knock on the door and do their dirty work with no one to stop them from stealing our babies right out from our breasts. We got to get in there now and get them kids back on the reserves.

RODNEY   Anne, my aunt once told me about this Cree girl that was taken out of her community when she was four years old and raised by white parents.

ANNE   Thieves!

RODNEY   And after ten years in court, her reserve got her
                returned.

ANNE   See, I told you it could be done.

RODNEY   Think about it. This teenager, raised in the city,
                forcibly taken from the white family she grew up
                with and loved, shipped off to this isolated reserve
                way up north, where she didn't know anybody, or
                even the language. She was living in poverty for
                the first time in her life. She didn't know how to
                relate, make friends, how to live. She didn't fit in.
                She was gang raped by a group of boys on the
                reserve. Nobody likes an outsider.

ANNE   Where was that girl's mother? Where was her
                family? That story should have been a happy story.
                That's not like me, Rodney. I'd make sure she fit
                in.

                BARB enters from the bathroom.

BARB   The first thing I want to do is plug that damn hole
                in the bathroom wall. Talk about freezing your
                balls off. Mom, can I borrow ten thousand?

ANNE   Oh leave me alone.

                BARB looks out the window.

BARB   We could put the satellite disc right up over the
                doghouse. Then maybe we could get a dog. Not a
                reserve mongrel, but one of those purebreds,
                something with class. (*her eyes light up and she
                relishes the words*) A pit bull. (*to her mother*) Oh,
                Mom, bring it out. Can I touch it again, huh?

                ANNE brings out the cheque.

ANNE   Until we figure out what to do with it, I'm going
                to put it away in a safe place.

ANNE gets up to put the cheque in a jar on a high shelf:

BARB   But, Mom! What if the house burns down or something?

ANNE reconsiders and climbs back down.

ANNE   I guess we should go see a banker or something tomorrow.

BARB breathes a sigh of relief. ANNE passes the photograph on the wall which slows her down.

ANNE   Time to come to my senses, too. I know I'm stubborn but it shouldn't take two dozen detectives to drill it into my skull. Court records are classified. Adoption records are sealed. There's no way of finding out. That was my last hope.

RODNEY   We put you on the adoption registry.

ANNE   I know what the chances are of anything happening with that. She probably doesn't even know it exists. I didn't. I wonder if she has a happy life.

BARB   I'm sure she did, Mom.

Infuriated by the past tense, ANNE looks at her daughter with rage, but the emotion slowly burns out. ANNE leaves the room. There is a terrible silence.

RODNEY   So what are you two fun-loving girls planning to do for Christmas?

BARB is still looking off after her mother.

BARB   Wanna help pick out the tree on Saturday? If you want, you can spend Christmas with us, too. Mom told me to ask you. You can help us do the tree on Christmas Eve.

RODNEY   (*backing off*) Now Barb, that's a family sort of thing.

BARB   (*bristling*) I take it you don't want to spend Christmas with us?

RODNEY   I have my own family, Barb.

BARB   It's not as if your family would miss you for a few hours.

RODNEY   Ah, I have other plans.

BARB   I see. Well, maybe you'll find the time to at least visit us on Christmas Day.

RODNEY   Don't be that way. I've got my reasons.

BARB   You've got excuses. Every time something comes up that's important to me, you make excuses.

RODNEY   For instance?

BARB   The tenth anniversary of my father's passing away. You didn't even bother to show up for the dinner.

RODNEY   That's not fair. I was busy.

BARB   You had a bowling tournament. A bowling tournament is not busy, it's an insult.

RODNEY   It was a curling bonspiel, not bowling!

BARB   Details.

RODNEY   And it was the league finals, too, Which goes to show what a great interest you take in what's important to me. It's getting late.

                 RODNEY turns to leave. BARB is disgusted.

BARB   You always do that.

RODNEY   Do what?

BARB   Wimp out in the middle of an argument. It drives
                  me crazy, Rod. You won't even stand there and
                  fight with me like a man.

RODNEY   I will argue with you, Barb. But I just don't see the
                  point of fighting about something, getting all
                  emotional over it. It just clouds the issue rather
                  than helping you reach any kind of understanding.
                  And besides, when you start a fight, you always
                  end up doing both parts yourself, anyway. I think
                  I'd better go.

BARB   Yeah, you'd better go. See ya.

                  *RODNEY opens the door to leave. BARB
                  follows him and looks outside.*

                  (*annoyed*) Great, it's snowing. Looks like it's going
                  to be an even whiter Christmas.

                  She slams the door behind him.

RODNEY   I get the feeling it's sure going to be a cold one.

                  (*moving out into the cold winter night*) I know
                  what you're thinking. Shallow, egocentric man
                  afraid of commitment. Oh, shut up. I have my
                  reasons, trust me, and they're good ones. So I don't
                  like Christmas, the once-a-year generosity and
                  syrupy good will, the sappiness. Ever wonder why
                  there are so many diabetics in the world? Even so,
                  I'm tired of being portrayed as Otter Lake's version
                  of The Grinch. I don't want to steal Christmas, I
                  just want to ignore it, but it won't ignore me.
                  (*starting to sing*) "You're a mean one, Mr.
                  Rodney." (*agitated*) My shoes aren't too tight. My
                  head is screwed on just right. And my heart isn't
                  two sizes too small. Bah humbug.

                  *

*Act Two: The reunion. ANNE grabs a cloth
and moves toward JANICE. She cups the
opposite side of JANICE's head with her hand,
wets a small part of the cloth with her tongue,
and wipes her face as if she were a child. The
closeness to her long lost child begins to affect
her. Her voice quivers, her heart is beating a
mile a minute. Even though the job is all
finished, she doesn't remove her hand. They
stare into each other's eyes, and ANNE slowly
pulls JANICE closer until they are hugging.*

ANNE   Grace...

        *ANNE pulls back slightly, tears in her eyes,
        and a little embarrassed. Too much too soon.*

ANNE   So many questions for you. Thirty-five years of
        questions.

JANICE   Me too.

        *The millions of questions go through each of
        their minds, each trying to figure out the
        appropriate first one.*

ANNE   Where did you grow up?

JANICE   In Southern Ontario, London actually.

ANNE   I've been there. Oh my, I could have passed you on
        the street. The people who raised you, what were
        they like.

JANICE   They took me around the world.

ANNE   Brothers? Sisters?

JANICE   Two brothers.

ANNE   Where were you in the family?

JANICE   They are both older. Gregory's in Germany right
        now and Marshall lives in Vancouver.

ANNE   Really, so far apart. Most of our family still live around here. Marshall and Gregory, huh? What was that other name you go by?

JANICE   Janice.

ANNE   That's a pretty name.

JANICE   Thank you. I was named after my mother's grandmother. She was a—

ANNE   You were named after Grace Kelly.

JANICE   I beg your pardon?

ANNE   Grace Kelly. You were named after Grace Kelly.

JANICE   I was?

ANNE   *Rear Window* was the first movie me and your father ever saw. You were born the year *High Society* came out. You were named after Grace Kelly.

JANICE   Grace Kelly. Interesting.

ANNE   I think she was one of the most elegant ladies I ever saw. I wanted my daughter to grow up just like her. Tall, beautiful, can look life in the face. And look, look at you, Grace.

JANICE   You've never seen me in the morning. I like her, too. What's your favourite movie of hers?

ANNE   Oh, High Noon for sure. I thought she was simply marvellous in it, just waiting around for Gary Cooper to get killed. Marvellous. Westerns have always been my favourites.

JANICE   Even the ones where the Indians get killed?

ANNE   Well, they weren't real Indians. What kind of movie do you like? Have you ever seen *The Magnificent Seven* with that bald-headed guy, what's-his-name?

JANICE   Yul Brynner.

ANNE   Yes, Yul Brynner.

JANICE   A long time ago. But I prefer the original, Akira Kurosawa's *The Seven Samurai*. You know, with Toshiro Mifune. I find it a better, more complex film.

ANNE   What year was it made?

JANICE   Fifty-four. Why?

ANNE   Must have missed that one in Peterborough. Maybe me and Barb will rent it sometime, *The Seven Salmon Eyes*?

JANICE   (*smiling*) Samurai.

ANNE   Samurai.

JANICE   It's one of my mother's...favourite films. She had actually studied in Japan for a number of years just after the war.

ANNE   She sounds like...an interesting woman.

JANICE   Oh, she is. I owe her a lot.

ANNE   I'd like to meet her.

     JANICE looks at her, surprised.

JANICE   You would?

ANNE   She's looked after my little girl all these years. Oh yes, I'd like to meet her. Oh, Grace, I gotta know. Are you married? Am I a grandmother?

JANICE   Sorry, no children, though I haven't quite ruled them out. I was married for two years but that was a long time ago. Too much business, not enough breakfasts for Eric.

	He decided to go off and cook for himself.
ANNE	He didn't like your cooking?
JANICE	Not much time for cooking. Work keeps me busy.
ANNE	A lawyer. My daughter the lawyer. Whatever made you become a lawyer.
JANICE	It's a tradition in the Wirth family.
ANNE	Do you enjoy it?
JANICE	That was hardly an issue. Doing well was. It seems in the world of the white middle class, Indians have a reputation for doing things half-assed.
ANNE	Some people do think like that, don't they? But there's nothing you can do about people like that.
JANICE	Oh yes, there is. Don't give them anything to be critical of. Be the best. Be untouchable. That's how you get ahead in this life. Even in private school, I tried for valedictorian, the best of the best. That June I wanted to be up there, on the stage, under the awning, while the other girls sat on the lawn getting sunburned.
ANNE	And did you?
JANICE	Came in second, and sunburned.
ANNE	Second is good.
JANICE	That's what my father said. but it wasn't good enough for me. If I'm in the system, I want to be in the system to win.
ANNE	You sound like someone from "Dallas" or "Dynasty".
JANICE	Yes, well, that's my life.

ANNE

You sound so lonely. I guess it must have been difficult for you. Was school hard on you?

JANICE

In some ways, not in others. On the volleyball team we were given names to be put on our jackets. I was Pocahontas. At the time I thought it was funny. I always knew I was an Indian, but it never actually meant anything to me. Just a fact of life, like being five foot seven. Then Meech Lake happened with Elijah Harper. And Oka. Suddenly everybody was asking me my opinion on this or that situation. They wanted the "Native perspective". But the only perspective I had was a suburban one. I started to wonder about my past, and the more questions I was asked, the more I had questions about myself. Finally, I had to know. I went to London, found the court I was processed in, got my adoption papers, contacted the Department of Indian Affairs, and they eventually told me what reserve I was from. I've had the information for a while. I was too...I guess frightened to call, then I saw your pictures in the paper about the lottery. Congratulations, by the way. Once I saw your faces, I knew I had to call. To meet you. And here I am. That's my life in a nutshell.

***

Blues For My Grandfather

Tien Providence

Tien Providence was born on the Caribbean island of Saint Vincent, and started writing in his teens, eventually publishing a book of short stories and poetry. His first play was "Shotgun Wedding", produced in schools on the island.

After moving to Canada in 1988, he worked for four years teaching drama, producing and directing theatre productions with the St. Vincent Cultural Group. In 1989 he published a book of short stories. He directed a production of "Weeds", by Tom Zeigler for The Theatre Group at the Annex Theatre, and in 1995 he directed "Blues for My Grandfather" at the Alumnae Theatre's New Ideas Festival.

Blues For My Grandfather

Tien Providence

*A self-contained monologue written for performance at
an evening of Caribbean voices, then performed at the
1995 New Ideas Festival at the Alumnae Theatre. It is a
story taken from the headlines, giving voice to the other
side. It highlights the pain, the sorrow and the anger
you feel when someone you love is shot down.*

> *Lights down, stage is dark. We hear the sound
> of a saxophone playing. Slowly a light shines
> on a chair positioned in the centre of a bare
> stage. From out of the shadows, a young
> person walks up to the chair, leans on it, stares
> out at the audience, slowly walks around and
> sits in the chair, then begins to speak.*

This used to be my Grandfather's chair.
Yeah! He used to love to sit here and tell us stories.
Funny stories, sad stories, (*smiling*) scary stories.
We used to scream, me, my brothers and sisters.
We'd all run off to our bedroom afraid to sleep.
But the next night, we'd all come back for another scary story.
Those were the ones we liked best, especially the one about how a
Lajabless nearly catch him in her trap.
You see them Lajabless is real pretty woman and they does always dress
up nice, nice in they long gown and thing.
But they does only dress up like that because one of they foot is a goat
foot.
So that is why they could only wear long gowns.
But anyway, he say is a good thing he was a fast man in he days or he
woulda get ketch.

He tell we he meet this woman one night on his way home from a party.
She looked so good that he decided, boy I got to try something. So he go
up to she and start to lay some serious lyrics on the lady.
"Man she was butter in my hand" he would say as they started to walk to
her house.
While they were walking, he decide to make his hand fast and next thing
you know, his hand was brushing against a hairy thing.
He realise that, is no way a woman leg supposed to have so much hair.
So out of curiosity he pull up the dress, quick, quick and he see the goat
foot.

Man, he say he tek off, he never run so fast from a woman in he life. A
man like he who was known as the biggest woman chaser in the village
was now running from woman.
We laughed until we cried, whenever he told us that story.

Those were the days before we got a TV and before he lost his mind.

You see after the TV came
We didn't listen to his stories as much.
After all we had something else
to hold our interest.
So after a while he joined us and the TV became his comfort too.
Especially the old western.
Oh how he loved those cowboy movies.
Sometimes he would fantasise.
My grandfather had a beautiful imagination
and that is why it happened.

One night he and his buddies were having a drink in one of the bars
around the place.
They were having a good time, talking about the old days (*laughs*) They
loved to talk about the old days in the West Indies.
I used to go with him sometimes when he visited his buddies and I would
sit and get completely wrapped up in the stories.
But anyway back to what I was saying.
This night, my grandfather was at the bar drinking and having a good
time, when some racist punks came by and started making trouble, calling
them old niggers and asking,
"Why don't you niggers go home and leave our country alone?"
Well my grandfather was a real proud man and nobody was going to call
him nigger for too long.
I wasn't there but I heard, he just lost it.

He got up and jumped into those guys like he was some cowboy hero. By the time the police got there he was well into taking care of them and you know who got arrested?

Sometimes in this place, if a Blackman and a Whiteman gets into a fight, it is understood that the Blackman gets arrested without question.

Being in jail broke my grandfather.
He had to stay there a few days because my mom didn't have the money for the bail.
So he had to wait until she could borrow it

My grandfather, a man who loved his freedom.
"His own way" my mom would say.
He just couldn't stand being in a cell.
He felt trapped like a bird in a cage.
So he caused quite a ruckus.
That is another cowboy word.
Anyway during one of these daily fights with the guards, he got shot.
It left him partially paralysed.
The guards said it was an accident but I believe differently.

My grandfather became a shell.
We couldn't reach him as he retreated more and more into his TV world.
His favourite chair; this chair was exchanged for a wheelchair.
He would sit in front of the TV for hours.
Sleeping and waking in front of it.

We left him alone because we didn't know what else to do and we couldn't afford expert help.
So we watched our grandfather trying to reach out but he couldn't.
Sometimes I would cry because I missed him.
I missed the stories, but most of all I cried because I was unable to help.
I felt so impotent.
Neighbours said we should put him in a home but we couldn't, we just couldn't.

Early one morning, trouble came. Big time.
Grandfather woke up in front of the TV as usual but something was wrong with the set that morning.
Cable must be down or something like that.
It just wasn't working.
My Grandfather started going off and creating such a stink.

We tried to calm him down but the more we tried the more he cussed and screamed.
One of the neighbours must have called the police because they were soon knocking down our doors.

They broke the door down and two big beefy white policemen with policesticks drawn entered.
They had a 'we'll take care of this' look on their faces.

They took over, ordered us out of the room.
In our own house. Imagine that.
We left. What else were we to do?
I half closed the door and peeked through the crack.

My Grandfather had quieted down a bit as he watched the police advance towards him.
I caught the glint in his eyes and I just imagined what was going through his mind.
He was probably in some kinda cowboy fantasy.
The police got closer to him and suddenly he lashed out and screamed, "No You'll never take me alive.
I'll defend this town to the very end."
Then he drew a fork. I don't know where the fork came from, maybe we had forgotten to pick it up when we took his tray away.
Now it was in his hand. He held it like he had a six-shooter and he started making popping sounds.
The police began to wrestle with him and for a moment all I could see was the wheelchair swinging right and left.

Left and right. My Grandfather was putting up a good fight for a half crippled man.
But then he was always a proud man.
I smiled and was proud of my grandfather.

I kept looking at the ensuing battle wanting to help but was too afraid to go out.
I watched as my grandfather pushed one of the policeman away from him and suddenly...

> *Shots ring out and the stage is plunged into darkness. A beat, then the spotlight comes up on the youth. He is kneeling and pounding the floor with his fists as he cries:*

NOOO. NOOO. Nooo.

You didn't have to kill him.
You didn't have to kill him.

> *The sax plays as the youth repeats the line*
> *over and over getting softer as the lights so*
> *down.*
>
> *Then the stage is brightly lit as the youth*
> *paces.*

We buried our grandfather amidst all the controversy.
We marched and demanded justice.
Big dream.
But we still marched.

The policeman was charged after much demonstration.
But it was all a sham.
The trial was a travesty of justice and the verdict needed no deliberation.
When the expected judgement was read the cop took out a cigar, lit it,
breathed a sigh of 'Thank you,' I suppose and said,
"I'll do it again, If I have to."

> *The youth walks a bit, stares at the audience*
> *and repeats the line.*

"I'll do it again."
What a thing to say.

***

Mom, Dad, I'm Living with a White Girl

Marty Chan

Marty Chan is a Canadian playwright whose work has seen great success from the Edmonton Fringe Festival to Toronto to Vancouver. In Toronto, the Cahoots Theatre/Theatre Passe Muraille co-production of "Mom, Dad, I'm Living with a White Girl", sold out a four-week run in March, 1995. Vancouver's Firehall Arts Centre mounted a second production of this play in February, 1996. One of his Fringe plays, *Polaroids of Don*, received an Edmonton Sterling Award nomination for best new work and best production. His commentary, "The Dim Sum Diary", which takes a quirky look at his Chinese family and how they became accustomed to living in Canada, is heard regularly on CBC Radio in Alberta. He also has a recurring role in the Canwest Global television series, "Jake and the Kid", adapted from W.O. Mitchell's short stories and radio plays.

Mom, Dad, I'm Living with a White Girl

Marty Chan

*Mark has a secret he keeps from his traditional Chinese
parents: he lives with Sally, a white girl. His fear that
his mom and dad will not accept her translates into
nightmares in the vein of racist films about the Yellow
Claw, a Chinese overlord who tries to rule the world.
Sally urges Mark to reveal the truth, but his nightmares
hold him back.*

*Act One, Scene One. A stage divided into
sections represents MARK GEE's twisted
world. A bed lays out intimacy and secrets. In
front of it, MARK GEE (22) stands with
SALLY DAVIES (24). Formality, lies and LI
FEN GEE (52) sit at a dining table. But she
sits in shadows so that only her long cigarette
holder is visible. At centre stage, a long bench
stands for truth, justice and the Chinese-
Canadian way. It also represents an
acupuncturist's clinic. On the wall behind, two
tasselled spears bracket a life-sized body chart.
Behind the bench, KIM GEE (53) holds an
Earth-like balloon. KIM slides a long cruel
needle across the balloon.*

KIM   The key is the entry point. Find the right one and
we can reach the nerve centre. Strike where they are
most vulnerable. Ah. The heart of decadence.
Toronto. We will infiltrate their society as a moth
chews through silk. They will suspect nothing,
Yellow Claw.

> *LI FEN flicks her cigarette. KIM inserts the needle. It pierces through the other side of the balloon. SALLY joins MARK.*

SALLY Black crows fly at midnight.

MARK The tall man ducks under the low arch.

SALLY Maple syrup flows in February.

MARK The cat is dead.

SALLY I despise smokers.

> *MARK lights a cigarette for SALLY.*

SALLY Did you uncover the Yellow Claw's secret plot?

MARK She has many secrets.

SALLY Agent Banana, the freedom of the western world rests on your shoulders. If you can't learn her plans—

MARK I know what's at stake, Snow Princess.

SALLY Redouble your efforts. We're counting on you.

MARK I won't let you down.

SALLY Good luck and God speed, Agent Banana.

MARK Save a drink for me Snow Princess. We'll toast an end to the Yellow Claw's tyranny.

SALLY To the unshakeable Rocky Mountains.

MARK To the Can in Captain Canuck.

> *SALLY grabs MARK and kisses him. Lights down. Lights up on KIM and LI FEN. Once again, she is hidden in shadows. Only her cigarette is clearly visible.*

KIM	One of your minions no longer inhales the Opium of a Thousand Loyalties. What is your wish?
LI FEN	A lotus blossom plucked from the garden of obedience will wither and die.
KIM	I hear and obey, Yellow Claw.
LI FEN	Amuse me with the name of my betrayer.
MARK	He is no one of consequence.
LI FEN	Tell me.
KIM	His identity slips my mind.
LI FEN	His name!
KIM	Mark Gee.
LI FEN	Bring him to me.
KIM	I faithfully do your bidding, mistress of evil.

Crash of gong. Lights up on bed. MARK sleeps. SALLY flips through a script.

SALLY	I can't believe the drivel some writers pass off as art. Listen to this title. Wrath of the Yellow Claw. Isn't that terrible?
MARK	Awful.
SALLY	Here's a good one. The Yellow Claw's influence undulated across the Pacific Ocean as a dolphin glides through the briny sea. But this was no playful fish. It was a dark porpoise.
MARK	Cheese deluxe. Can I read it after you're done?
SALLY	Why do you want to?
MARK	It's funny.

SALLY   Please.

MARK   I take it you're passing on it.

               A phone beside SALLY rings. She looks at it,
               but doesn't answer. MARK doesn't budge.

MARK   Let it ring.

SALLY   It might be important.

MARK   Let the machine get it.

SALLY   Mark, answer the phone.

               MARK picks up the phone.

MARK   Hello? It's midnight. Yes, I know about dinner.
               No, I don't need a reminder. Yes, I'll be there.
               Tomorrow night. Seven-thirty. Seven. Got it. You
               don't have to call again. I'll remember. Good night.
               Good night. Good bye.

SALLY   Your Mom?

MARK   Who else? Man, I wish she'd stop doing this.

SALLY   It's the Dragon Boat Festival. It's important to her.

MARK   Yeah, this and a thousand other obscure Chinese
               festivals.

SALLY   Maybe we can watch the boat race this year.

MARK   Are you nuts? Mom would want to throw
               dumplings into the sea, and you know how Dad
               can't stand to see food go to waste.

SALLY   Neither can you.

MARK   I wish she'd stop making excuses to get me to
               visit.

SALLY   She cares about her *sai j'i* (little boy).

MARK	I'm not her little boy.
SALLY	I love it when you try to be tough.
MARK	I am tough. Not an ounce of fat.
SALLY	Except right here. (*tickling him*)
MARK	Cut it out, Sally. I mean it. Stop it.
SALLY	It's from all those years of eating war tips.
MARK	That's *waw teep* (dumplings). You make it sound like I sucked on missiles.
SALLY	Okay, waw teep. Better?
MARK	Yeah.
SALLY	Are we going to tell them tomorrow?
MARK	It's too soon.
SALLY	That's what you said last time. Mark, they need to know about us.
MARK	Trust me, I'll know when to do it.
SALLY	We have to tell them some time.
MARK	Not yet.
SALLY	Why not?
MARK	It's my Dad. He's got a weak heart.
SALLY	But he seems so healthy.
MARK	It's in our genes. Grandpa Gee died of one.
SALLY	I thought you said he lived in Calgary.
MARK	He did, but now he's dead.

SALLY   When did it happen?

MARK   A while ago. Two, maybe three months. I'm not sure. Dad has the details.

SALLY   And we didn't attend the funeral?

MARK   Dad hasn't put the body into the ground yet. He and Grandad never really got along.

SALLY   What are you scared of?

Clash of small cymbals. MARK hands SALLY a cigarette.

MARK   We shouldn't have succumbed to our primal desires. Sweet is the fruit that is forbidden. Snow Princess, you are my queen. My little banana. Um, maybe we should drop our code names.

SALLY   Call me Sally.

MARK   Mark.

SALLY   A strong name. Like Mark Antony. Slayer of Caesar. Ruler of Rome. Consort of Cleopatra.

MARK   Sally. Sally. Sally.

SALLY   No one must know of this. It could ruin us both.

MARK   Your secret is safe upon my lips. Let us seal them.

They lean in to kiss. KIM enters.

KIM   The Yellow Claw sends her greetings.

MARK   No.

KIM flicks his hand. SALLY clutches her chest. She pulls out a throwing star.

SALLY   Smells like highly concentrated opium. It will knock out an adult in three sec— unh!

MARK   Sally? Snow Princess? Wake up. (*to KIM*) What do
            you want?

KIM   You are guilty of consorting with the white devil.
            What have you told the infidel?

MARK   I won't talk.

KIM   You will break like so many Taiwanese toys.

            *KIM throws a star at MARK. He falls. Crash
            of gong. KIM exits. SALLY and MARK sit
            up.*

MARK   I just think we should wait.

SALLY   You have no idea how they'll accept the news.
            They might be fine with it.

MARK   Not Mom.

SALLY   She is a reasonable woman.

MARK   Dream on. She's the original dragon lady.

SALLY   Don't say that. It's racist.

MARK   You don't know my Mom.

SALLY   Mark, it'd be nice to get better acquainted with her.
            You know, invite her to visit us for a change.

MARK   How come you're so fired up to tell her?

SALLY   I'd like to answer the phone once in a while.

MARK   We'll get call display.

SALLY   Development likes their readers to be somewhat
            accessible.

MARK   We'll get a second phone.

SALLY   Mark, it's more than that. I'm still dressing out of my suitcases. I'm not paying rent so I can live out of boxes.

MARK   Give them a chance to get used to you. Just like your opa warmed up to me.

SALLY   He still calls you China Boy.

MARK   At least he doesn't ask me to break boards any more.

SALLY   That was Uncle Wes.

MARK   Sorry, they all look alike to me.

SALLY   I was proud to tell my parents.

MARK   And they took it so well.

SALLY   Mark, what's the real reason you're lying to your parents?

MARK   It's Mom. I wanted you to get on her good side before we said anything.

SALLY   You don't think I've been trying? I offer to help in the kitchen, she sends me away. I practise a few words of Cantonese, she laughs.

MARK   Compliment her food.

SALLY   She never accepts my praises.

MARK   Its just Chinese humbleness. Lay it on thick, no matter what she puts in front of you.

SALLY   Your Mom's cooking is always delicious.

MARK   She's taken it easy on you. One day, she's going to cart out her mystery dish. Woof woof.

SALLY   Please stop that. You sound like my opa.

MARK   You'll try to get on my Mom's good side?

SALLY   I can't earn her respect with this lie hanging over
            us. We have to be honest up front.

MARK   But you haven't given this lying thing a fair shake.

SALLY   Promise me. Tomorrow night.

MARK   Just remember to lay it on thick with the food.

SALLY   I'll insist everything's delicious.

MARK   Do it until she chokes on your compliments.
            Hmmm.

SALLY   Mark.

MARK   A boy can dream, can't he?

            *Lights down. Chinese percussion sticks beat
            rapidly.*

                        ***

The Madwoman and the Fool: A Harlem Duet

Djanet Sears

Born on the cusp of Leo and Virgo, in London, England, Djanet Sears accounts for the breadth of her accomplishments as writer, director, actor and singer by blaming it on the stars. She describes herself as a woman of African descent, and speaks colourfully of the enormous move her family made from London to Saskatoon, when she was barely 15 years old. Having survived life in the prairies, Ms Sears felt well prepared for virtually anything — especially life as an artist. Her plays include "Who Killed Katie Ross", "Afrika Solo" for stage and for radio. Published work also includes "Naming Names: Black Women Playwrights in Canada" in Women in the Canadian Stage. "Afrika Solo" won both the International Armstrong Award for Outstanding Radio Play, and the International Radio Festival of New York, Silver Prize.

The Madwoman and the Fool: A Harlem Duet

Djanet Sears

*This is a play about Shakespeare's Othello and his first
wife, Sybil (Billie), before he married Desdemona. It is
set in contemporary Harlem. The other characters
include Magi, the landlady of the building where
Othello and Billie live, and Canada, Billie's father.*

BILLIE

I thought I saw them once, you know. On the subway. I had to renew my
prescription. And I spot them. He and Her. Something...sharp forces air
out of me. My chest is pounding. My legs can't move. From the back, I
could see the sharp barber's line, separating his tightly coiled hair from
the nape of the skin at the back of his neck. His skin is soft there...and I
have to kick away the memory nudging its way into my brain. My lips
on his neck, gently...holding him — don't, don't, don't, don't, don't. O.K.
O.K. Here, before me — his woman — all blonde hair and blonde legs.
Her weight against his chest, His arm around her shoulders, his thumb
resting on the gold of her hair. He's proud. You could see he's proud. He
isn't just any Negro. He's special. That's why she's with him. And
she...she...she flaunts. Yes, she flaunts.

They are before. I am behind, stuck there on the platform. My tongue is
pushing hard against the roof of my mouth...trying to hold up my brain,
or something. 'Cause my brain threatens to fall. Fall down through the
roof of my mouth, and be swallowed up.

Slowly, slowly, I press forward, toward them. I'm not aiming for them
though. I'm aiming with them in mind. I'm aiming for beyond the yellow
line, into the tracks. The tunnel all three of us will fall into can be no
worse than the one I'm in trapped in now. I walk — no, well hover really.

I'm walking on air. I feel sure of myself for the first time in thirteen weeks. Only to be cut off by a tall grey man in a police uniform, who isn't looking where he's going, or maybe I'm— maybe he knew my aim. He looks at me. I think he looks at me. He doesn't say a word. He brushes past. Then a sound emanating from...from...from my uterus, out of my mouth shatters the spell. They turn their heads — the couple. They see me. It isn't even him.

I run...run...run home. And take thirty-three aspirin, small and white, clean and bright, spread in neat rows along the kitchen counter. Only to heave them up, the aspirin, caught like half dissolved stars, in a wash of bile on the floor.

I'm not crazy. I know I'm not crazy. But it worries me — I mean...sometimes it's difficult to grasp. Not so much that I might want to die. I don't. I'm already dead. Something has been murdered in me. What worries me — I mean...I...I...I may actually have been willing to commit murder.

*

OTHELLO

You don't want the truth. You want me to tell you what you want to hear...No, no, you want to know the truth? I'll tell you the truth. I prefer White women because you are the mirror of my ugliness. Yes, White women *are* easier — before and after sex. They want me and I want them. They aren't filled with hostility about me, about the unequal treatment they're getting at their jobs. We make love and I fall asleep not having to beware being mistaken for someone's inattentive father. I can explain that I'm confused with every lousy lover, or husband that had ever left them lying in a gutter of unresolved emotions. That's the truth. To a black woman, I represent every black man she has ever been with and with whom there was still so much to work out. The white women I loved saw me — could see. Look, I'm not a junkie. I don't need more than one lover to prove my manhood. I have no children. And I did not leave you, your mother, or your aunt with six babies and a whole lotta love. I am a very single, very intelligent, very employed African American male. And with White women it's good...it's so nice, and with Mona because even at birth, she had that constant half-smile, like the Mona-Lisa. Skin as smooth as monumental alabaster...as warm snow velvet. Her silken hair...in my arms. In her bed. She sees me...as a man. Other women I've been with can only appreciate a fraction of what it means for me to present a steady and solid direction — White women appreciate it more often. They're used to it as a history. Anyhow, we're all equal in the eyes of God, aren't we? Aren't we?

*

MAGI

George and I, we'd been seeing each other the better part of...what...two years. I'm just not getting any younger. I mean, I kept dropping hints I was ready for him to pop the questions. Seems like he don't know what question I'm referring to. So I decided to give him some encouragement. See, I've been collecting things for my trousseau, and I have this negligée...all white, long, beautiful lacy thing. Looks like a see-through wedding dress. So, I'm out on the balcony — you know, 'cause it's too hot inside, and I still ain't got around to putting in air conditioning. Anyway, I see him coming up the street. So I rush in and put on the wedding-dress negligée, thinking he'll see me in it, all beautiful like — want to pop the questions, you know. So I open the door, me in the negligée, and he... He just stands there. Mouth wide open. When finally he does speak, he says, he guesses he should go get a bottle of wine, seeing how this was gonna be some kind of special occasion an all. Now I don't know whether he got lost...or drunk...But I ain't seen or heard from him since.

*

MAGI

Oh no, no, no. You know what I hate about Christmas? Seven days to New Year's Eve. And I hate New Year's Eve. And you know what I really hate about New Year's Eve? It's not the being alone at midnight. It's not the being a wallflower at some bash, because you fired your escort, who asked for time and a half after 10 p.m. It's not even because you babysat your friends kids the previous two. I really hate New Year's Eve because it's six weeks to Valentine's Day. Well, maybe that's too strong. No. I really hate it. What I really hate about Valentine's Day is...it's my birthday. Don't get me wrong now. I'm glad I was born. But I look at my life — I'm more than half-way through it, and I wonder, what do I have to show for it?

*

CANADA

The first time I came to Harlem, I was scared. Must have been '68 or '69. Yeh... We were living in the Bronx, and your mother was still alive. Everything I'd ever learned told me that I wasn't safe in this part of town. The newspapers. Television. My friends. My own family. But I's curious, see. I say Canada, you can't be in New York City and not see Harlem. So I make my way to 125th. "A" train. I'm gonna walk past The Apollo, I'm gonna see this place. I'm gonna walk the ten city blocks to Lexington and catch the "D" train back, if it's the last thing I do. So out of the subway, I put on my 'baddest mother in the city' glare. I walk — head straight. All the time trying to make my stride say "I'm mean". "I'm mean. Killed somebody mean". So I'm doing this for five, ten minutes, taking short furtive glances at this place I really want to see, when I begin to realize...no-one is taking any notice of me...not a soul. Then it dawns on me: I look like I live in Harlem. Sounds silly now. But I just had to catch myself and laugh out loud. Canada, where did you get these ideas about Harlem from? Who was this information meant for? Clearly not you. But then who?

*

CANADA

(*talking to BILLIE*) I nearly came before...two or three times...you know, when I heard. I wished your mother was here. I really wished for her...her wisdom. I mean she'd know what to do. A girl needs her mother. And I know you didn't have to tell her all those times...I mean, I couldn't tell you. What could I tell you? I kept seeing your face. It's your mother's face. You've got my nose. My mouth. But those eyes...the shape of your face...the way your head tilts to one side when you're thinking or just listening. It's all her. You've got her moods. I used to call them her moods. Once, 'bout every three months, on a Friday, when she'd have the weekend off, she'd come home from that hospital, take off her clothes and lay down in her bed and stay there 'till Sunday afternoon. She'd say she'd done turned the other cheek so many times in the past little while, she didn't have no more smiles for anybody. She'd say, better she just face God and the pillow than shower me and the children with the evil she had bottled up inside her. So I'd take you and Drew and we'd go visiting. We'd take the whole weekend and visit all the folks we knew, in a 15 mile radius.

See, if you spend much time among White people, you start believing what they think of you. When we'd get home, she'd have cleaned the house, washed the clothes, and even made Sunday dinner. And after I'd pluck the guitar...and she'd start to sing...and you'd dance. You'd stomp on that floor like you were beating out some secret code to God or something...I know you — we don't see eye to eye. I know you haven't wanted to see very much of me lately. But I've known you all you life. I carried you in my arms and on my back, kissed and spanked you when you needed, and I watched you start to talk, and learn to walk, and read and I just wanted to come...I just wanted to come and I know I can't make everything all right. I know...but I was there when you arrived in this world...and I didn't think there was space for a child, I loved your mother so much. But there you were and I wondered where you'd been all my life, like something I'd been missing and didn't know I'd been missing. And I don't know if you've loved anybody that long. But behind you mother's face you wearing, I still see the girl who shrieked with laughter and danced to the heavens sometimes.

***

The Mercy Quilt

Lorre Jensen

Lorre Jensen is a Toronto playwright whose works include: "The Mercy Quilt", produced for CBC Radio Stereodrama; "The Shaman of Waz", Playwrights Workshop Montreal; "Pen Pals", Nightwood Theatre, Toronto; and "Coming Around", co-written with Paula Wing, Theatre New Brunswick.

The Mercy Quilt

Lorre Jensen

*In this scene from the radio play, GRACE nurses some
maternal grief that her only child, LORRAINE, has
'never been asked' and begins to explore the reasons for
this oversight.*

Scene 16.

Sound: knock at the door, door opens.

GRACE   Lorraine?

LORRAINE   What is it, Ma?

GRACE   Let me sleep with you tonight.

LORRAINE   Sarah scared you, huh?

GRACE   Sarah's been scaring us all since we were girls.
               Tell me about the city.

LORRAINE   What do you want to know?

GRACE   Were the people nice?

LORRAINE   Some were.

GRACE   What about the white people?

LORRAINE   That's who I meant.

GRACE   Did you have friends there?

LORRAINE   Of course, I had friends, Ma.

GRACE   Any men friends, I mean?

LORRAINE   Some were men.

GRACE   White men?

LORRAINE   Aren't you sleepy?

GRACE   And you didn't meet one you wanted to marry?

LORRAINE   You wouldn't have wanted me to marry a white
                    man, Ma.

GRACE   Well, only as a last resort. It's better with your
                    own kind.

LORRAINE   I want to march to my own drum, Ma. Not
                    somebody else's.

GRACE   You left it too long.

LORRAINE   No, I've always been that way. Maybe because I
                    was the only one.

GRACE   I couldn't conceive of any more.

LORRAINE   One was enough, huh?

GRACE   I believe we raised you right.

LORRAINE   Of course, you did.

GRACE   To be kind to others and not think only of yourself.

LORRAINE   Marriage is more than an act of kindness, Ma.

GRACE   It's a hundred acts of kindness every day, going
                    back and forth between husband and wife.

LORRAINE   What about love? Look at Sarah.

GRACE	Sarah's been sweet on Handsome since she was in pigtails. Still carrying the torch and the man's been gone nearly ten years. (*pause*) There's a lot of widowers on the reserve.
LORRAINE	Like Isaac?
GRACE	Yeah.
LORRAINE	He's an octogenarian.
GRACE	What's wrong with that?
LORRAINE	Nothing. I just don't want to marry one.
GRACE	Course. I think Kathleen's got her eye on Isaac. Was it a white man?
LORRAINE	Who?
GRACE	The man who asked?
LORRAINE	There was no man.
GRACE	You said there was.
LORRAINE	I know. Because I think it disappoints you that I wasn't asked.
GRACE	I wasn't asked either.
LORRAINE	Go on!
GRACE	No. I saw that everybody around us was getting married so I said to your father: Bull, looks like we're the only single ones left. What d'you say we get hitched?
LORRAINE	What did he say?
GRACE	(*mimicking BULL*) Good idea.
LORRAINE	That's it? That's all he said?

GRACE   He wasn't big on words.

LORRAINE   Were you afraid of getting left behind?

GRACE   Seemed like such an awful thing for a young girl.

LORRAINE   You think it's awful for me?

GRACE   You got no one and when I'm gone—

LORRAINE   Ma?

GRACE   Yeah?

LORRAINE   Don't be sorry for me.

GRACE   Is that why you said you were asked?

LORRAINE   In a way and I didn't want you to be sorry for you either, because I think you take it personally that I wasn't asked. Sometimes it's kinder to hold back the truth.

GRACE   You must have learned that in the city.

LORRAINE   I'm learning it from you.

                              *

Scene 22.

GRACE, MARGE and SARAH, led by LORRAINE
who is GRACE's girl and newly arrived from the city,
seize an opportunity to look for the missing beads.

	Doorway to MAY's house. Sound: door creaks open, radio is playing, "Delilah" by Tom Jones.
LORRAINE	The door's open.
	Sound: muffled footsteps as women enter.
GRACE	Who's that singing? Sounds like that guy always giving away his clothes.
	Sound: the radio volume is lowered. Music: flute presence.
LORRAINE	That's better. Okay. Let's look for the beads. Try not to move anything. What's the matter, Ma?
GRACE	We need a pie.
LORRAINE	No, we don't.
GRACE	Be better if we had a pie.
LORRAINE	Ma, we didn't break in. The door was open.
MARGE	Look what's here. The picture we had taken with our first quilt. Must be near forty years ago.
GRACE	Let me see.
MARGE	There's Kathleen and there's you, Grace. Remember your permanent wave? Look Sarah, here you are.
SARAH	Something's wrong.

LORRAINE	What is it, Sarah. You should come away from the door, just in case—

Sound: rustle of feet.

SARAH	I don't see May.
GRACE	May wasn't born when we had this picture taken, was she, Marge?
SARAH	I don't see May out on the bay. She just disappeared, like, swallowed up by the water.
LORRAINE	Don't say that, Sarah.

Sound: muted turtle rattle.

GRACE	Take a picture of this, will you? Our prize beads lying here on this old trunk!
MARGE	Let me see.
GRACE	Let's make a run for it. Here. You take the beads, Sarah.
SARAH	The turtle's gone.

Flute punctuates the idea. Sound: car engine is heard faintly.

LORRAINE	Somebody's coming. Geez, it's the police!

Sound: mad scramble to hide. Eager footsteps scurrying.

GRACE	The jig's up!
LORRAINE	Just sit down.

Sound: scramble to chairs.

LORRAINE	Stay quiet. If he comes in, I'll say we're waiting for May to come with our fish.

> *Sound: engine stops. Car door opens and
> closes, footsteps on gravel, a knock on the
> door and the pounding of a heartbeat. There is a
> second knock, the heartbeat is louder.*

POLICE VOICE   (*muffled*) Hey, May? (*pause*)

MARGE   Answer the door, Lorraine.

LORRAINE   Ssssh. He's looking for May.

POLICE VOICE   (*muffled*) May?

MARGE   You better answer the door

> *Sound: door opening.*

Scene 23.

> *The front door of MAY's house. Sound:
> exterior sound, a car passing on a gravel road,
> faint sound of water*

LORRAINE   Hi! You looking for May? She went fishing.

POLICE VOICE   You're Grace's girl.

LORRAINE   That's right.

POLICE VOICE   You visiting May?

LORRAINE   Just waiting for her. She's getting me a pickerel.

POLICE VOICE   Give her these, will you? Say, are you the one
selling the raffle tickets?

LORRAINE   Why?

POLICE VOICE   The wife was telling me. Said you got some artist
to make a necklace.

LORRAINE   That's right.

POLICE VOICE   You got any left? The wife's birthday's coming up. I might get lucky and win it for her.

LORRAINE   I think so.

POLICE VOICE   Can you come to the station?

LORRAINE   Now?

POLICE VOICE   No. Not right away.

LORRAINE   Okay. I'll...give these to May.

POLICE VOICE   Sure thing. You know, I was thinking... (*pause*)

Sound: heart pounding rises briefly during pause.

POLICE VOICE   There's a guy at the station...he's single too. We kid him about it. Says he's waiting for the right one.

GRACE   (*whispered*) Who's he talking about?

POLICE VOICE   Somebody in there with you?

LORRAINE   It's my mother. She's waiting for a catfish. I'll tell May you came by.

POLICE VOICE   Okay.

Sound: door closing.

***

The Sniffer

Marvin Francis

Marvin Francis' roots extend to Heart Lake in northern Alberta. He started writing at an early age. (Translation: "I made comic books and forced younger brothers to buy them.") He has written for the stage and radio as well as some puppetry plays. He studied Theatre and English at the University of Winnipeg and is an active member of Sage Story Tellers, an aboriginal writer's group based in Manitoba.

The Sniffer

Marvin Francis

A dingy alley. It is the '90s. Jake, a businessman,
Halley, a preacher, and Delores, an academic come upon
Julius, who is sniffing glue out of a plastic bag.

JULIUS

My universe is contained in this plastic. It's a floating world. It's a world that only I can enter. The fumes have colour, have sparkles, have this whiteness closing in, like a cocoon, man, like a womb. The fumes surround me with their whiteness.

JAKE

Get a job! You need a job! Be like me. I'm so happy!

HALLLEY

Listen to me! I am the word of God. God flows through me. Don't be a loser.

DOLORES

I'll bury you in books! Words will rip at your mind! Listen to me!

JULIUS

(*sniffing glue*) AHHHH! All is good now. The walls of the plastic bag are coated with sparkles. My mind sparkles. The colour is good. The walls are white.

JAKE

There's good money in glue. Lots of repeat sales. Listen to me, son, don't be an abuser. Sell to them!

HALLEY	Climb up here on this pedestal, you loser. Be in charge. Be the boss! God will let you. Be like me. I am blessed.
JULIUS	Who are these people? Why do they yell at me? Can't they see I am happy? In my world with its white walls. The colours of my mind mixing with the white walls; running down my nose. I'm happy here. Leave me alone!
JAKE	What's the use? He's beyond help. He's another statistic. He will cost us all money.
HALLEY	God is too busy for the loser. God is too important. I know. He told me.
DELORES	Words cannot reach him. Words are too important for this loser.
ALL	Let's show this bastard whose in charge. How dare he ignore us? Kick the shit out of him!

They start to kick and beat him.

JULIUS	Ow! Ouch! Arghhhh! I knew this was going to happen. Every Christmas is like this. Ow! Ouch! Where's my white wall? It's supposed to protect me. Where's my glue?
HALLEY	Kick him in the face! God told me.
JAKE	Get his wallet!
DELORES	Study him. Dissect his loser mind.

Silence.

HALLEY	He's not moving.
JAKE	He has no wallet?
DELORES	He's..he's...
HALLEY	A fucking loser! Who cares? Not God.

JAKE	Look at him. Dead with a smile. Can you believe that?
DELORES	Why would this loser smile?
HALLEY	Wait! God is talking to me. God is telling me...(*pause*)...he died because he loved those white walls.
JAKE	That makes no financial sense.
DELORES	Maybe white walls don't sneer.

They leave JULIUS in the alley.

***

Riot

Andrew Moodie

Born in Ottawa, Andrew Moodie has been an actor for many years. He has written two plays, "Hysteria" and "Riot". He is currently living in Toronto and writing his next play.

Riot

Andrew Moodie

This is a play about the changing nature of Canada, set in the black community of Toronto during the Rodney King trials in Los Angeles. This scene is the opening of the play.

> *Act One, Scene One. As the house ligths come down, the preshow music crossfades to Gil Scott Heron's "Peace Go With You Brother". Lights come up on stage to reveal GRACE at the dining table studying. EFFIE is on the couch, wrapped in a blanket, watching TV, eating Doritos. The music continues. EFFIE slowly stands, points the remote at the RTV. The lights and music fade.*

WENDLE   Fuck Quebec!

> *Lights up. WENDLE and GRACE are at the table. The table is cluttered with their text books and note books. EFFIE is laying on the couch reading a paperback. The TV is off.*

GRACE   Quebec is a distinct society!

WENDLE   What the fuck makes them a distinct society?!

GRACE   The French language and culture.

WENDLE   Being a black man from Nova Scotia does that not make me distinct?

GRACE   Yes, you are distinct, but that doen't stop them
             from being distinct.

WENDLE   Look, you know me. I love Brain Mulroney, I
             voted for him, I supported the Free Trade
             Agreement, so did people in Quebec, they're not
             afraid to compete in a global market, he's from
             Quebec, I recognize that....it's not that I don't like
             people from Quebec, it's just that when they try to
             tell me that they are better than me, I get pissed
             off.

GRACE   They're not saying they're better than you, they are
             looking for the tools to ensure their culture.

WENDLE   Jean Chretien is French! He's from Quebec! He
             doesn't seem to think that we are destroying French
             culture.

GRACE   Look, I have friends back in Montreal who would
             tell you that Jean Cretien is a brown-nosing two-
             faced Unce Tom opportunist who will lick English
             Canada's asshole so that one day he will become
             Prime Minister.

WENDLE   You are seriously fucking deluded.

GRACE   I'm just telling you what some people are saying.

WENDLE   Well look, if you're French and from Quebec at
             least you have a shot at becoming Prime Minsiter.
             They're ain't going to be no Black Prime Minsiter
             here in Canada within my life time and you know
             it.

GRACE   You got me there. Fine.

WENDLE   Maybe they should stop thinking about their own
             culture for a moment and think about other
             cultures, like what thy're doing to Native people!

GRACE   Oh, come on!

WENDLE	The French are the most racist, bigoted people in the world.
GRACE	Bullshit!
WENDLE	You go to those people in Oka, you go tell the Mohawks how wonderful Quebec culture is!
GRACE	Don't you dare try and tell me that the people in Quebec are so racist, but hey, Nova Scotian's love Native people, Nova Scotian's don't have a racist bone in their body!
WENDLE	Quebecers are more racist than people in Nova Scotia.
GRACE	(*louldy*) You've never lived in Quebec! You have no idea...
WENDLE	(*loudly*) They had slavery in Quebec!
GRACE	(*loudly*) They had slavery in Nova Scotia!
WENDLE	Okay, look, you want me to feel sympathy for Quebec, why should I feel sympathy for Quebec?
GRACE	It's not a matter of feeling sympathy for Qauebec...
WENDLE	Then what is it?
GRACE	1804 to around 1805 there was a crop failure in Lower Canada. This lead to lumber production becoming the number one export to England. With increased export there came with it increased immigration from England. These newly landed immigrants were shocked that the French played such a large role in the civil service, and the French were shocked that the English came to dominate the eocnomy. This is the source of Quebec nationalism pure and simple. Soon political parties were split along ethnic lines and paved the way for the rebellion of 1837.
WENDLE	I...

GRACE   Just shut up and listen to me for a second.

WENDLE   Don't tell me to shut up.

GRACE   Pierre Bedard, leader of the Canadian party was
               arrested along with other editors of the party
               newspaper for simply discussuing French
               Canadians being in charge of their own
               government. When Joseph Papineau became leader
               of the paty, he organized a rebellion to take Lower
               Canada away from the British. Their initial victory
               at St. Denis was followed by losses to the British,
               culminating in the defeat at St. Eustache. Ever
               since that defeat, Quebec nationalists have dreamed
               of an Independent Quebec, with a declaration of
               independence, and...this is what drives me crazy
               about you Canadians! You should learn your own
               friggin' history!

WENDLE   Well...they better stop complaining and learn to
               speak English and like it because it is the
               international language of business, and that's it.
               And when I go to those French stores, they better
               speak to me in English and they better like it!

GRACE   Why would a Quebec poet need to speak the
               international language of business? Why would a
               cattle farmer in Frontenac need to learn the
               international language of business.

WENDLE   I don't care if you're Chinese, Portuguese, Italian,
               French or what the fuck...I'm in your store? Speak
               to me in English.

GRACE   Okay, fine.

WENDLE   It's the international language of business. You
               learn it, you speak it and you like it!

GRACE   I am so glad we are no longer going out together. I
               swear to God.

                              ***

The Troubleshooter
Alicia Payne

Alicia is a professional actor and an emerging writer, "Yo, Canada!", her first full-length play, was developed while participating in the Playwrights Union of Canada Writers' Circle '95. It was selected for further development in Nightwood Theatre's Groundswell Workshops.

In 1995, Alicia received a Heritage Canada bursary to participate in a screen-writing course at the Summer Institute of Film and Television. She developed her improvisational writing and acting skills in The Second City Training Centre, and also the 1993/94 Master Class showcases. In 1994, Alicia was a contributor to Horrorscope, a syndicated cartoon which appears in *The Toronto Star*.

As a professional actor, Alicia's credits include theatre, film, television, video and radio. She is a member of the Black Film & Video Network, Canadian Actors Equity Association, Canadian Artists Network; Black Artists in Action and Theatre Ontario. Currently, Alicia is participating in a writer's triad at the Black Film & Video Network.

The Troubleshooter

Alicia Payne

*Old-school discipline meets New-Age understanding and
a student with capital 'A' attitude. With the help of a
guidance counsellor, a principal tries to resolve a
conflict between a teacher and a student.*

	LUNA CYCLE - a guidance counsellor, VIRGIL TATTLE - a techer, WADE WEIGHED - a high school principal, SHANIKA - a student. The setting is the student lounge. LUNA and WADE gesticulate when speaking.
LUNA	I've been a guidance counsellor for over 20 years. The times have changed.
VIRGIL	Wade, it's insane to be holding this meeting in the student lounge. We're just sitting ducks.
LUNA	We must reach out to her and all the students like her. Sometimes all we need to do is meet them on their 'turf' as they sometimes call it.
WADE	Luna has a point. Continue.
VIRGIL	We shouldn't have a student lounge. This is where they plot to overthrow us, you know.
LUNA	In order to make contact, we need to speak in a lingo to which she can relate.

VIRGIL	I told you she'd be late. We shouldn't even be having this meeting. Just put her out on her ear. No questions asked.
LUNA	Relax Virgil. You'll make her defensive. It's not like she committed some criminal offence.
VIRGIL	It wouldn't surprise me if she did. We should save some innocent person from becoming a victim by sending her to prison now, before she gets a chance to commit a crime. That's if she hasn't already.
WADE	Now Virgil, that's hardly fair. After all, we still live in a democratic society.
VIRGIL	Well, we shouldn't.

SHANIKA enters.

VIRGIL	You're late, Missy.
SHANIKA	I know all us students look alike but my name's not Missy.
WADE	Good afternoon, Shanika.
LUNA	Yo! What's up?
VIRGIL	Don't get smart. You're late.
SHANIKA	Oh.
VIRGIL	What have you got to say for yourself?
SHANIKA	Niente. That's Italian for nothing.
VIRGIL	Why you—
WADE	Let's get started shall we.
LUNA	I like your outfit Shanika. It is so cool!
SHANIKA	Thanks. Man.

LUNA	Please, call me Luna. We're all friends here.
WADE	Perhaps you'd be more comfortable seated.
VIRGIL	She's fine right where she is.
LUNA	Chill, Shanika. Take a load off...your feet.
VIRGIL	Don't get too comfortable. We're going to suspend you. That should make these hallways a little safer to walk.
WADE	May I remind you, Mr. Tattle, that this is just an informal meeting to see if we can reach some mutual understanding.
VIRGIL	What's to understand. She's a bad student and a bad influence on everybody who knows her.
LUNA	Let's avoid labelling. It encourages a negative mindset.
VIRGIL	Look here, Luna psycho.
WADE	Mr. Tattle, Ms. Cycle, let's have some order shall we. Now, on to the business at hand.
VIRGIL	Hah! She doesn't even have the decency to stay awake for this meeting. This is what I have to deal with in class.
WADE	Shanika? This is hardly appropriate behaviour.
SHANIKA	I'm not asleep Mr. Weighed. This is just a very comfortable position to sit in.
VIRGIL	It's disrespectful is what it is. How can you learn sitting like that? Can you imagine if I taught in this position?
LUNA	It's unorthodox, yes, but let's avoid hasty judgement. We must allow for individual expression. People learn in different ways.

VIRGIL	Learn nothing. She sleeps in homeroom and now she's lying to cover her tracks.
LUNA	You're labelling.
SHANIKA	Look. You want to suspend me? Suspend me. I don't have time for this.
WADE	Wait a minute, Shanika. This isn't a trial. We're just trying to understand why you're having difficulty in school.
SHANIKA	You're right. I'm not on trial. (*reaching into her pocket*) You are.
VIRGIL	I told you she was trouble.
LUNA	Stay cool, Girlfriend. Stay cool.
SHANIKA	I knew I'd be outnumbered so I brought a little insurance, if you know what I mean. Don't worry. I'll only use it if you make me. Let's play a game. Let's play school. I'll be the teacher.
VIRGIL	I won't play. I won't I won't I won't.
SHANIKA	I'm the teacher. You do as I say.
LUNA	Role reversal. What a useful counselling tool.
SHANIKA	Ms Cycle, please put up your hand when you wish to address the class.
VIRGIL	Wade, do something.
SHANIKA	Tsk, tsk, tsk. I see you need to practice putting up your hand before you speak, Mr. Tattle. Put up your hand.
WADE	(*raising his hand*) Your point is well taken, Shanika. May we continue?

SHANIKA	Well, class. Mr. Tattle seems to think he makes the rules around here. Looks like I'll have to make an example of him. Again. Put your hand up and keep it up until I say you can take it down.
	VIRGIL raises his hand.
SHANIKA	(*beat*) Is that your interpretation of up? That's better.
VIRGIL	It's getting tired.
SHANIKA	My, we're forgetful today. Since one hand was already up, you should have raised the other hand in order for me to realise you wanted to address the class. This calls for a detention.
LUNA	(*raising a hand in a gesture*) Go, girl!
WADE	(*raising a hand*) This is quite remarkable.
VIRGIL	This is—
SHANIKA	Oh...
VIRGIL	(*slowly raising the other hand*) May I please lower my hands now, Sir — Ma'am? I have learned my lesson and I apologise to the entire class for wasting valuable learning time.
SHANIKA	Very well, Mr. Tattle. You may lower your hands but you must still serve your detention. I have an engagement this evening so we'll start it right now. You can stand with your face against the wall. Take your notebook with you so you can jot down the assignment.
LUNA	This is very revealing.
SHANIKA	(*removing a tape recorder from her pocket*) By the way, I am recording the class in case any of you were planning to have memory lapses about whether I in fact gave the class an assignment.

WADE	Well, my eyes have been opened.
SHANIKA	Today's Social Studies assignment is radically different from what you're used to but I have renewed faith in you.
LUNA	I'm going to suggest we do this at the very next conference.
SHANIKA	This weekend, I'd like you to make an effort to communicate with someone with whom you think you have absolutely nothing in common.
WADE	What a brilliant assignment.
SHANIKA	Instead of written reports, we'll take some time over the next week *listen* to your experiences. Have a great weekend. Class dismissed. Not you, Mr. Tattle.
WADE	Thank you for enlightening us, Shanika. I'm going to personally review your assignments and re-evaluate your grades.
SHANIKA	Thanks, Mr. Weighed. Mr. Tattle didn't want to teach me. And when I did well on assignments he accused me of plagiarism and failed me anyway so I stopped trying.
WADE	Mr. Tattle?
VIRGIL	There may be some truth in what she said.
LUNA	(*exiting*) Shanika, let's catch a slice...of pizza. I'd like to rap with you some more.
SHANIKA	Sure. Cool.
WADE	I think you have a lot of reflecting to do, Virgil. Stay there until I come back for you. (*exiting*)

***

The Strength of Indian Women

Vera Manuel

Vera Manuel is Shuswap-Kootenai from the interior of British Columbia. She is the eldest sister in a family of four sisters and five brothers, and is aunt to 21 nieces and nephews. She is a graduate of the University of British Columbia, and works as a National Trainer/Facilitator, Writer, and Curriculum Developer in the areas of family systems, sexual abuse healing, personal and professional development in the Aboriginal community.

She has written two training manuals for counsellors, "In the Spirit of the Family" (Native Family Systems), and "The Right to be Special" (Sexual Abuse Disclosures in the Aboriginal Communities), and is currently developing a third, focused on providing support, encouragement and counselling for First Nations Youth. Vera also works as a playwright, poet, and storyteller, and has written and produced two plays which deal with issues of concern in First Nations communities.

The Strength of Indian Women

Vera Manuel

Ever since the 1880s, governments have tried to forcibly destroy Aboriginal culture and assimilate Native people by removing children from the community and putting them in residential schools. Attendance was mandatory and anyone who refused was jailed and the children removed by force.

Beatings for speaking their own language, saying their own prayers or running away were often accompanied by the horror of emotional, physical and sexual abuse. As children were the heart and soul of the Aboriginal community, it only took a few generations for this community to break down and for the evils of the residential school to manifest themselves on the reserve. This play illustrates the tremendous will of Aboriginal people to survive and overcome these abuses. When the women tell their stories they open the doors back to the future generations, and they unlock the chains of the past.

MARIAH

I get afraid to talk. All my life people tell me, "be quiet, shut up, don't say nothin'." Even the old people before used to say to me, "don't tell stories...if you attack the church, you make hard times for everybody." Now, I'm old, and I keep my mouth shut, and still we have hard times. It's gettin' harder and harder. Sousette, it's gettin' harder for ever'body.

I don't know why the Lord guided me back to this place, or even why I should still be livin' and all these other women are dead. I keep askin' the

Lord ever'day, "what is it that I need to do?" and I hear nothin'...just those dreams that won't allow me a decent night's sleep.

I know there are those of you who believe I don't belong here. For most of my life I've wanted to believe that too. It's always been so easy for me to leave here, to tune away from that side of me that's Indian...except it's like turnin' my back on the only human being who ever truly loved me...my gran'ma who was Indian told me once, that it was not going to be easy livin' on the edge of two worlds, and I see that now, when my eyes are open...that this has been true.

When I walk in the Indian world I hear them tauntin' me.

> *MARIAH covers her ears, moves about, very distracted, trying to flee the sound of those cruel voices from childhood.*

"Teacher's pet, teacher's pet. Hey little white girl, whatta you doin' 'round here? Are you a little wannabe? Are you one of those Bill C-31 Indians?"

And when I walk in the white world I hear them taunt me.

"Little Indian Squaw, why don't you go back to the reservation where you belong. Hey Pocohontas, are you a little Indian princess? You're not really like one of them, you're almost white."

> *MARIAH stands determined, she is not going to run anymore. She is going to face those ghosts, no matter how painful and frightening they are.*

Well, almost is not good enough. I've come home to find out who I really am. I knew who I was when I was a little girl livin' in my titti's (grandmother's) house, before they took me away to that school. I knew who I was when she would light the juniper and guide my tiny hands over the smoke, pulling it up over my hair...across my heart...and down the rest of my body. She would turn me in a circle, always to my right, and she would tell me that the Creator gave me as a special gift to her, to watch over her for a time. That, at that time, I was the most perfect, and precious thing, there was no doubt. I believed that with all my heart.

What I seen in that school shocked me into silence and disbelief in everything that was good.

*MARIAH paces, wringing her hands, very
agitated, afraid to tell, but she knows she
must. She stops suddenly and speaks very
clearly.*

But it was not the Lord that did that, I know that now. It was just people
like you and me.

*MARIAH still struggles to tell the story, her
whole body is agitated and grieving. She is so
afraid that she may be betraying God in the
telling of her story, but she cannot hold it in
any longer.*

I saw that girl, Theresa, refuse to stop speakin' Indian, refuse to quit
prayin' to Napika (the spirits)...I saw her always encouragin' others not to
forget they were Indian, and I admired her strength, and the depth of her
determination. While no one else spoke to me...I had no friends, you
see...she would always stop to give me a kind word, and I grew to love
her like the older sister I never had. I'd sneak her extra food, she'd break it
into bits and share it. I saw her challenge them again and again, daring
them to do what they finally did to her...silence her. I saw Sister Luke —
hate and venom spewing out of her mouth, "You dirty, savage Indian,"
she spat, and pushed that Theresa down, down two flights of cement
steps, and I said nothin'. My screams were silent, and my agony and terror
all consuming.

I saw murder done in that school, and when they wrapped that broken
body and sent it home to the mother, tellin' her it was pneumonia that
killed her little girl...she unwrapped it, and runnin' her grievin', lovin'
mother's hands across the bruised face, shoulders, legs and back,
discovered the neck was broken, screamed out in agony, "No...why? What
has happened to my baby?" I said nothin'.

I saw little girls takin' in the night from their beds. I heard the moans and
groans and sobbing. "Shut up! Shut up!" I cried. Glazed eyes, ravaged and
torn bodies returned in a frightened, huddled mass beneath the sheets,
and...I said nothin'.

MARIAH feels the need to justify her inaction.

You're a good girl, they told me, these girls are bad, they need to be
taught a lesson.

I saw a baby born one night to a mother who was little more than a child herself. I saw her frightened, dark eyes pleading with me to save her child...then later when the grave was dug, and the baby lowered into the ground...I said nothin'.

> *MARIAH turns her back, which is bent as though crushed by the weight of this story. Slowly, she begins to straighten her back and, turning to face the audience, she explains her transformation, and visually we see her transformation as she purges herself.*

When my gran'ma died I was only nine, and I had no one. At Christmas and summer holidays, no one came to claim me, so "they" became my family. They stroked my light skin, and brushed my brown curls, and told me I was almost white. They pampered and spoiled me, and there was not a place in that school that I was not welcome. I had special privileges, and, because I was so good at sayin' nothin', I became one of them. I was very loyal. When I left that school, Father placed this gold cross around my neck, and he cried, and wished me well...made me promise to come back and visit...

...I walked away...never looked back, not once. For a long time after that I couldn't pray, and for years I believed in nothin'.

***

Body Blows

Beverley Yhap

Originally from Trinidad, Beverly Yhap is a graduate of the
Fine Arts programme at York University. She was founding
Artistic Director of Cahoots Theatre Projects in Toronto and is
currently based in Vancouver, and working on her new play,
"Hope Sing". Her other plays include "Body Blows" and
"Settlements".

Body Blows

Beverly Yhap

Years earlier, Lydia betrayed herself for Jason,
sacrificing all ties to her family and culture, exiling
herself from the sources of her power. In this country,
she is feared as different by everyone including her
adolescent daughter. Lately, she has begun to suspect
Jason of cheating. After lengthy avoidance, they are
brought face to face with the rift in their marriage.

LYDIA and JASON in bed. Both toss and turn.
Suddenly JASON touches his face as if hit by
something. He pulls the sheet over his head, but this
doesn't stop the water.

JASON   (*swats another drop of water*) Stop...

                   LYDIA pushes back the sheet, sprawls across
                   the bed. JASON dodges another drop.

                   Dripping...faucet..? (*looking up and getting a series*
                   of drops in the eye) Shit!

                   He covers himself and moves away from the
                   damp near LYDIA.

LYDIA   (*half asleep*) What?

JASON   Stay on your side...

LYDIA   (*waking*) Why...the wet...coming from?

JASON   Go to sleep.

LYDIA	(*awake*) Is raining...where the storm?
JASON	It's nothing. It'll peter out...
LYDIA	Jason. Get up quick!

LYDIA gets up quick. JASON remains fixed.

The bed soaking wet.

JASON	I have to decide.
LYDIA	Get a pail — quick.
JASON	I put off and procrastinated.
LYDIA	Talk sense, Jason, don't only—
JASON	The problem is — there's never a good time.
LYDIA	Don't rile me, Jason.
JASON	There's always some crisis...
LYDIA	At least ease yourself off and move that side.
JASON	No.
LYDIA	You think you special or what, eh?
JASON	I'm an asshole...and I'll take my time deciding...just how—
LYDIA	Far you can push me...with these stupid antics of yours?
JASON	Sure, insult me. You're not goading me into...
LYDIA	Since when I goad you to do—
JASON	I should've punched you out long ago. Then it wouldn't have to come to this.

> *Flabbergasted, LYDIA sinks onto the bed,*
> *inadvertently right in the wet. Water starts to*
> *pour onto the floor gradually making a pool.*

This...slow, steady pace.

LYDIA
You hear what you just say?

JASON
The water's just starting to pool out on the floor..

LYDIA
Stop this pretence...

JASON
The water's real Lydia. The water's forcing me...

LYDIA
This waterfall of crocodile tears...

JASON
Fuck off. I'm not jumping for you. This is
happening...the way it's happening...and I'm not
doing a thing to speed it up.

LYDIA
So there! You spite yourself if all we drown.

JASON
Sure, sure, up the ante. (*beat*) You're just going to
have to wait...if it breaks you.

LYDIA
Fuck you, Jason. You better had decide...if you
bailing out or what...

JASON
I'm not bailing out. You think it's my fault? I'm
doing this on purpose?

LYDIA
You mean it's an accident...pure coincidence?

JASON
I've been avoiding this...

LYDIA
I know you like a book, Jason.

JASON
I don't want you to read into events — get too
literal. So here we are...I'm an idiot — trying to
hold back...

LYDIA
You and Hercules...holding the weight of the world
on your shoulders...

JASON	It had to be something drastic—
LYDIA	For who, Jason?
JASON	It had to be a flood.
	Water is everywhere.
LYDIA	For you...you always go overboard.
JASON	It's the only way I know with you.
LYDIA	Only, you stop short of the truth.
JASON	Lydia, I've tried.
LYDIA	You do damage, don't blame it on me...
JASON	I tried for Jay-Lynne's sake.
LYDIA	Stop trying so hard.
JASON	I never wanted this to happen.
LYDIA	If you going, go overboard.
	LYDIA shoves JASON into the water.
JASON	Once and for all..
LYDIA	That's only the beginning...
JASON	I've had enough, Lydia.
LYDIA	Only the surface of you wet and shiny...
JASON	I used to be comfortable—
LYDIA	Everywhere deserve a good drowning...
JASON	When did it start to slide? When did mess start to...seep in? Fifteen years is too long to lie down, dry and easy in that bed.

LYDIA	The bed we made together.
JASON	The bed I could lie in, did lie in — easy. Till now.
LYDIA	Toss and turn, you mean, don't deceive yourself.
JASON	I'm out from under, I'm exposed, damp, in deep—
LYDIA	Where? You want to see deep?

> *LYDIA shoves JASON onto his back in the water.*

JASON	You kick me—
LYDIA	Tired of you stirring up the surface...
JASON	I'll kick back!

> *A water fight breaks out with JASON kicking water at LYDIA. She kicks back, he grabs her leg and pulls her down.*

Stay still! (*splash*)

LYDIA	(*big splash*) No, you!
JASON	Whatever happens...
LYDIA	Let go!
JASON	I get Jay-Lynne.
LYDIA	Wash your face!
JASON	I'm serious.
LYDIA	You hear me joke?
JASON	I have every right.
JASON	(*simultaneously*) She's my daughter.
LYDIA	(*simultaneously*) She's my child.

LYDIA	You want...let's saw her in two.
JASON	I want what's best for her.
LYDIA	She belongs to me.
JASON	That's not how it works.
LYDIA	I'm her mother.
JASON	Lydia, I don't want a war.
LYDIA	All of a sudden, she so precious to you...
JASON	I was hoping we could talk reasonably.
LYDIA	You have to go and open up a flood?
JASON	You have to understand. I didn't set out to hurt you.
LYDIA	You aim good then.
JASON	It just happened. I couldn't help it.
LYDIA	(*simultaneously*) Don't tell me was Destiny.
JASON	(*simultaneously*) It was meant to be.
JASON	I wasn't even looking—
LYDIA	To my face, Jason.
JASON	It's the truth.
LYDIA	No more dodging around behind my back—
JASON	We just happened. Don't you remember?
LYDIA	No more cover up, masquerade—
JASON	You're shivering...

LYDIA	I remember...like yesterday...the words you mouthed like vows...
JASON	Why do you do it? Why do you drag up the past like a dirty secret? I was there. I know when it started to change.
LYDIA	I see you from a distance, long time...from afar.
JASON	When forever started to deteriorate...go downhill...
LYDIA	Oceans where the eyes belong...
JASON	It's when you began to change.
LYDIA	Teeth wide as the shoreline...
JASON	You became different.
LYDIA	Regular....or Juicy fruit?
JASON	You weren't the same.
LYDIA	Taste the difference.
JASON	I don't know you anymore.
LYDIA	The flavour difference.
JASON	Nothing's the same.
LYDIA	Chew Juicy Fruit if you want to chew gum.
JASON	Everything's different. Isn't it?
LYDIA	Everything is you, you mean?
JASON	This old picture Jay-Lynne dug out of somewhere...I couldn't believe my eyes. Who the hell was that anyhow? I couldn't recognise those kids...it was jarring. I looked at you — and I look at you now, and it's two different pictures...

LYDIA	One of us stay constant.
JASON	Meaning what?
LYDIA	You know what is the difference between true and false?

Pause.

JASON	I want out, Lydia.
LYDIA	True or false?
JASON	What's the difference?
LYDIA	Over a picture?
JASON	All right...it's not the whole story—
LYDIA	It better had be more...
JASON	We have differences, Lydia. Major divides. For years, I'd try and paper over them, try and close a path—
LYDIA	But wait. We worlds apart — we be so from day one. The only difference now is—
JASON	Now. Not then...not time, not climate, not circumstance, culture, the whole nine yards. (*beat*) Not even June.
LYDIA	You so sure?
JASON	She's extraneous.
LYDIA	You let the cat out of the bag, Jason—
JASON	It's me and you—
LYDIA	Don't blame me if—
JASON	It's me. I grew it...built it up too long. Now it's crashed and look at the mess...I don't know...I was

helpless — paralysed — didn't know what to do — who to turn to—

LYDIA   So you went and fucked around.

JASON   Let's not get into accusations.

LYDIA   You only want to bring up differences to escape—

JASON   No, that's not what — you're not listening.

LYDIA   Toss and turn all you want, Jason. Different this, different that...when all you want is to trade in the old witch—

JASON   Lydia, I've been through hell to get here—

LYDIA   Hell? You better careful what you say, Jason—

JASON   Listen to me! If there's a way I can make it up to you.

LYDIA   I might have to do something.

JASON   I'm prepared to make a generous settlement.

LYDIA   Do some damage now for certain.

JASON   As long as you co-operate...

LYDIA   You hear *me*, Jason. Toss and turn your back on me now and you find out how much I change...with time. (*beat*) I did think — once upon a time — you were kind, I was the vicious one. I was the one deep in blood. It was a good masquerade. But now get old and used, you want to throw me away for good?

JASON   You make me hard and cruel standing up to you like this. Do you think I want to do this? (*beat*) I have to fight. I have to fight the fact that I still care about you.

LYDIA   Don't!

JASON	Fifteen years isn't yesterday.
LYDIA	Dry your conscience out elsewhere...
JASON	Do you know how hard loving you is? A lifetime's work...
LYDIA	Some hole don't have an echo...
JASON	You make it harder all the time.
LYDIA	Before I get my hands on you...
JASON	Now I want my life back.
LYDIA	Force you to recall just who it is you owe your life to!
JASON	You want to chain me to the past, for one set of events—
LYDIA	Not any old chain of accidents—
JASON	Back then, back there. I've moved on...
LYDIA	You profited...
JASON	You came along for the ride...
LYDIA	I burned all the bridges.
JASON	(*shrugs*) You did what you did.
LYDIA	I paid for my Destiny.
JASON	(*shudders*) You and fucking destiny.
LYDIA	Destiny was suppose to be a prize...
JASON	Fucking millstone of a curse. Your destiny. What about mine? I want one of my own. Is that so evil...I have to...
LYDIA	Shed blood...break bones...yes, in all...

JASON   Why? (*beat*) Isn't this damage enough?

LYDIA   No.

JASON   Why can't I go? Why can't I reason with
you...Can't you see? It's impossible...(*beat*) I don't
love you, Lydia...

LYDIA   I know...who you love.

JASON   Then...why hang on? (*beat*) You can't be...shit.

LYDIA   Don't worry, Jason. I'll manage. I'll find a way.

JASON   You...harm June and I swear — I will, I'll protect
her. You won't hurt her.

        Pause.

LYDIA   Is not she gun suffer. (*beat*) Is you...

        JASON exits.

        ***

This Is For Aborelia Dominguez

Monique Mojica

Monique Mojica is a Kuna and Rappahannock actor and playwright based in Toronto. Her performance credits include, "The Rez Sisters", "Jessica", "The Tempest", "Street Legal", CBC's "Conspiracy of Silence", and "Four Direction" Series. She can currently be seen in her third season as the Host/Storyteller on Vision TV's "Creation" and as 'Mad Etta' on CBC's "The Rez". Monique's play, "Princess Pocahontas and the Blue Spots" was produced by Nightwood Theatre and Theatre Passe Muraille in 1990 and published by Women's Press in 1991 along with her radio play "Birdwoman and the Suffragettes: A story of Sacajawea", which was produced on CBC Radio's Vanishing Point. Ms Mojica was the guest editor for the *Canadian Theatre Review* special issue on Native theatre, Fall 1991. Her short script, "A Fast Growing Mold Bitter As Shame" is published in *Gatherings*, vol. III *The En'owkin Journal of First North American Peoples*, 1992 and was produced by Ground Zero Productions as part of "Stolen Lands: 500 years +3", which Monique co-directed with Steven Bush.

Monique has recorded with Juno nominees, Kanatan Aski, Ulali, Jani Lauzon and Lawrence Martin.

Ms Mojica is a former Associate Director of the Centre for Indigenous Theatre and co-directed a residency program in Native Performance Culture at the Banff Centre with Floyd Favel.

This Is For Aborelia Dominguez

Monique Mojica

On January 12, 1994, a photograph of a Mayan woman
appeared on the front page of The Toronto Star. *Her*
name is Aborelia Dominguez. She comes from the
same territory as my husband. I had been there, I had
loved ones there who were afraid of the federal army. We
are "Indios", after all. As an Indigenous woman, my
memory of genocide is long. It is a grief I cannot yet
put down. The annihilation is happening now.

A face in a photograph

A headline

> "Revolt
> Rebellion
> Insurrection
> Uprising
> Rebels/peasants/Indians
> Mexico's Dirty War".

The bodies of two tiny girls; naked and stiff as broken baby dolls lie in
the corner of the photograph

> "...a horrible unearthly whitish-blue..." the caption
> says.

> I am crying.
> I am standing in a corner variety store crying,
> surrounded by potato chips.

The Korean woman at the counter looks
from me to the photograph
from me to the photograph
and shakes her head.

This is for Aborelia Dominguez

I need to say your name aloud
Tatsi'ants Mayan woman. Exposed in your grief; you turn your back to
death.

You could be Tzotzil, Tzeltal, Ch'ol, Tojolobal.
Blue shawl wrapped around your legs
blue blouse where you are holding your hand to your chest.
You have a Chamula face
and your dead daughters could be mine.

The people.
They are killing the people.
The genocide so clear
this time
again.

           I sat in those mountains
           in front of an auntie's adobe house/drinking posol
           from a gourd/
           the cornfields hanging off the mountains around
           me.
           Those mountains offer no refuge now.
Bomb and strafe.
Strafe.
           I didn't even know what the word meant
           but the Innu know,
           here,
           in their northern land.

Military aircraft flying low enough to graze the tops of the frozen bush;
the cornfields.

           White flags, diapers, scraps of clothing waving

STRAFE.

In the mountains
fleeing
ahead of the army

STRAFE.

twin baby girls forced from their mother's womb

This is for Aborelia Dominguez

My friends call:

Did you see the front page?
"I cried" she says, "standing by *The Toronto Star*
box"

My friends call:

Did you see the front page?
"I cried" she says, "Why didn't someone pick up
the babies and give them to her?"
We are crying.

This is for Aborelia Dominguez

I need to say your name aloud

And when the history is written of the
New Year's Day rebellion of the
Zapatista Liberation Army,
who will tell the story of
Aborelia Dominguez?

And when I sing the Strong Woman's song
it is for you
And if I sing a warrior's song
it is for you

This is for Aborelia Dominguez
This is for Aborelia Dominguez
This is for Aborelia Dominguez

This is for Aborelia Dominguez

All my relations

***

afrocentric

David Nandi Odhiambo

David Nandi Odhiambo was born in Kenya and studied at McGill University in Montreal. He currently lives and writes in Vancouver.

His works include a video collaboration, "Skinned" - screened at the Museum of Modern Art in New York, and a novel entitled,"up the lisping staircase". A segment of the novel was published in the December, 1995 issue of *Blood and Aphorisms.*

His work has appeared in *Tickle Ace, Absinthe, Reverse Shot Magazine, West Coast Line,* and *Diaspora.* David is currently working on a second novel.

afrocentric

David Nandi Odhiambo

The play examines the social, economic and cultural forces which bring a Black woman of mixed heritage and a Black man together, and the issues which subsequently tear their relationship apart.

Edah is from a wealthy family which has instilled in her a motivation to gain stability through education and marriage. Kiente, on the other hand, is from a poor family with similar values but whose existence has become a losing battle against poverty. They meet in their early thirties. Edah is married to Stanley, a white car salesman, and Kiente supports his own family by working as the couple's gardener.

> *Scene 1. Acid jazz plays as two blue spotlights light the stage. The music fades and lights dim. At stage left is a riser set diagonally, two chairs, an ashtray and bag next to the leg of one chair, with a torn brown blanket draped over the back. At stage right is a second riser covered in large intricately designed pillows, and a tall candle holder with three burning candles.*
>
> *EDAH enters, taking the room in. A noise startles her. She freezes before proceeding cautiously downstage, where she leans into the audience with a finger to her lips.*

EDAH   shhh

> *She looks around, walks to investigate a corner upstage, then walks up onto cushions.*

EDAH

going back
going waaaay back
there was a horse buggy on a highway
and a family worn/ drawn/ tired/ hanging legs down
out the buggy's back
hanging heads down too

She sits down, wraps the blanket around her
shoulders and gets comfortable.

this was my family
my great gran family worn and drawn and tired
fleeing
mud splattered on pant legs
a dirty brown blanket wrapped around shoulders
all eyes to the pebbles crushed by wooden tires
making tracks on the road
a black man/ a white woman/ and a mixed baby
my great gran family searching out a place
a peaceful place to explore deepening feeling

She wraps her arms around her legs, drawn up
to her chest.

it was cold
chilly to the bone
wind cutting through the brown blanket through
brown mud baked clothing

A loud noise brings her to her feet, startled,
dropping the blanket. She looks around before
tentatively settling back into her seat. She
reaches shakily into the bag, pulling out a
pack of cigarettes and nervously lighting one.

the horse up front
plodding through puddles
picking
cantering
at will
nobody telling it where to go
it just going any which way
stopping for some grass on the side of the road
stopping

rain beginning to fall
the baby crying
n' great granma
snot n' rain dripping at her nose

three next to broken
living from moment to moment holding on
next to broken
just holding on

> *She sits looking off into the distance, her
> cigarette burning down in her hand. She hears
> approaching footsteps, drops the cigarette to
> the floor hurriedly, stands to snuff it out, then
> gathers herself to hide behind a chair.*

*

> *Scene Four. EDAH takes KIENTE'S hand. She
> pulls him gently to lie with his back to the
> cushions and she shifts to sit up beside him.*

EDAH   i didn't like you at first

KIENTE   i didn't like you either

EDAH   i didn't like you more

KIENTE   i thot you wuz stuck up

> *EDAH pulls her hand away.*

EDAH   typical

KIENTE   typical/ what do you mean typical

> *EDAH stand to face him with her hands on her
> hips.*

EDAH   i mean typical black male reaction to any black
woman with a sense of herself

KIENTE   huh/ this wasn't sense of self/ you were all attitude/ like you were the only black person who knew what wuz goin on

EDAH   like i said/ typical

KIENTE   n' what about you

EDAH   what about me

KIENTE   treatin' me like i was some kinda black fool

EDAH   i didn't treat you like a fool

KIENTE   yes you did

EDAH   i didn't/ i just didn't trust you that's all/ you seemed to constantly be judging me for being with a white man/ waiting on some kind of explanation/ acting like i was yours cause i was black

KIENTE   that's not it/ that's not it at all (*as she turns to march out of the room, he moves quickly to stand in front of her*) don't go edah/ that's not what i meant/ i put it awkwardly/ i'm tryin' to say that isn't where my head wuz at (*facing each other for a short time, he points to the cushions*) could we sit down/ i'd like to talk about it but i'd feel more comfortable if we were sitting down.

     EDAH hesitates, then walks to sit in one of the chairs. KIENTE registers frustration.

EDAH   well

KIENTE   (*walking to her as he speaks*) i didn't get it/ that wuz all/ i didn't know what you were doing with him/ your haltin conversations/ talkin about escrow n' mortgage payments all the time/ (*stopping and putting both hands on the arms of her chair*) n' so much tension/ what was that

EDAH	kiente/ you exaggerate/ we had a hell of a lot more than that/ and anyway/ what relationship doesn't have tension
KIENTE	well (*stepping back to look at her*) whatever it was/ you certainly weren't very passionate together
EDAH	(*sharply*) we were passionate (*quickly softening*) we were/ in the beginning/ but we just got busy/ it happens/ n' you grow n' what you have is different/ that's all

KIENTE reaches for her hand.

KIENTE	you don't believe that
EDAH	i do believe that (*as he rolls his eyes to the audience*) what in hell was that
KIENTE	what
EDAH	that (*imitating him*)
KIENTE	i didn't do th...
EDAH	yes you did/ dismissing me as if you know me better than i know myself
KIENTE	edah
EDAH	no/ i'm tired of your looks and continuous corrections kiente

She sits on the chair and reaches into the bag for a cigarette. He walks over to sit on the cushions.

EDAH	i tell you what i believe/ n' you contradict me without an ounce of credit for having thought these things through
KIENTE	i didn't mean it that way
EDAH	you never mean it that way

KIENTE   wait a second/ you're constantly contradicting me too

EDAH   what

KIENTE   you just finished insisting that i acted like you were mine cause you were black/ when that wasn't what happened

EDAH   (*grappling to find the word*) that isn't analagous

KIENTE   yes it is (*facing each other in the smoke-filled silence, he adds quietly*) christ, do you have to smoke

EDAH   (*inhaling on her cigarette and blowing the smoke at him, then quietly*) n' do you have to be so controlling

KIENTE   o.k./ o.k./ if there was still passion between the two of you/ how do you account for what happened between us

EDAH   how do I account for it/ that's kind of a huge question don't you think/ I mean (*pausing*) how would you

                       He rises slowly, moving sexily to her and gently massaging her shoulders. She resists at first. He kisses the back of her neck, then works his way up to nibble on her ear. She laughs, falling back into his arms.

         so why did you do it

KIENTE   what do you mean why did I do it

EDAH   I mean/ why did you get involved with me

KIENTE   (*reaching out to tickle her stomach*) isn't it obvious

EDAH   stop (*pushing his arm away*) i'm serious

KIENTE   (*moving away sexily*) because you're fly

EDAH	that's weak
KIENTE	you are serious aren't you (*sighing and pulling away*)
EDAH	yeah/ I want to know/ the truth
KIENTE	god/ the truth/ I don't even think I know what that is anymore
EDAH	and kiente/ don't try to finesse me either
KIENTE	o.k./ the truth (*taking off his shoes*) the way you looked had something to do with it (*searching for the words*) yer lips yer hips yer all that booty (*indicating that "booty"*) the way you'd shimmy walkin' halls/ yer shyness hidden by an earnest seriousness (*still grappling for words*) the way the sun was on your naked belly/ the brittle timbre of your deep/ deep lipspeak (*thinking for a moment*) and yes/ perhaps anger as well/ I couldn't stand stanley/ or wuz it what he represented/ he wuz so self-assured actin' like his money gave him the right to do or say anything he pleased/ he kept sayin' he understood black people/ n' held up your marriage as some kinda proof/ but you weren't black (*getting a look from EDAH*) or/ at least those weren't the terms you both related to (*reaching up for a drag from her cigarette*) and it got to me thinkin' about slavery/ n' liberals n' whether it wuz possible for white people to ever really be connected to black people/ you know/ deep in the experience of blackness
EDAH	go on
KIENTE	anyway/ I didn't really think about it too much/ although it doesn't sound that way
EDAH	(*stubbing her cigarette and walking over to the cushions, with ashtray and cigarettes*) it had to do with race then

KIENTE

no/ there wuz somethin' else/ somethin' movin' deep inside of me that made me wanna take you away from where you were/ perhaps to show you things could be better/ not perfect/ but they would be better with me

> *EDAH smokes during an extended silence between them.*

EDAH

so it had something to do with who was a better man/ you the gallant black patriarch/ or him/ white wealthy n' insensitive/ (*breathing deeply*) that's messed up/ it's just stereotyping/ the stuff of bad political speeches and lousy...sexist fiction

KIENTE

(*turning to her in anger*) that isn't what i'm saying

EDAH

it damn well sounds like what you're saying

KIENTE

you're reducing what i've said to something entirely different from its original meaning

EDAH

n' you're being exasperating

KIENTE

hey wait a minute (*marching quickly to sit beside her*) wait a minute/ what about you

EDAH

don't change the subject

KIENTE

don't avoid the question/ why did you get involved with me

EDAH

(*playing with her cigarette and not looking at him*) boredom

KIENTE

boredom

EDAH

yeah/ boredom/ I was restless n' bored (*as KIENTE turns his back on her*) should I continue

> *Pause. He nods as if to say "Knock yourself out with it."*

EDAH

i'd surrounded myself with all things I thought would make my life complete/ a faithful husband/ a stable environment complete with deck chairs by the pool/ but something was still missing/ I was getting restless with where my life was at/ things were at such a standstill with stanley

he'd come home/ we'd eat supper/ i'd talk about my work or the people we both knew/ but there was no connection/ nothing real seemed to be happening between us/ soon we'd argue/ about his friends/ or the things we'd done or hadn't done to one another/ constantly having to explain ourselves over n' over again/ inevitably feeling guilty n' hopelessly understood

KIENTE

so I wuz just a pleasant distraction

EDAH

no/ not really (*trailing her toe along the side of his leg*) you see i'd never been with a black man before

He gets up abruptly and stands between the chairs.

n' here (*slowly walking toward him*) here was a fine looking/ soft-spoken brother whose movement was a slow hit of snaking rhythms, riffs n' licks

She reaches up to undo buttons on his shirt. He doesn't face her as she touches the skin on his chest.

n' whose black skin was the subtle hues of bruised n' disquieted evening sky/ perhaps I felt myself getting in touch with something intensely familiar with you

KIENTE

damn it edah/ a curiosity

He slaps her hand away and sits on the cushions.

EDAH i'm only being honest/ although i'm not certain this was the way I saw events were happening then/ it's how I see them now/

She walks toward him again and takes his head in her hands. He resists her at first but after some coaxing moves to kiss her as she pulls away from him. She pulls him down toward the floor and they pull at shirts and belts.

n' how it started one grey wet afternoon/ tripping clear I asked you to give us a kiss

KIENTE (*laughing*) n' I spilt the tea I was drinking down the front of my shirt

EDAH n' I could breathe freely again/ it was as if we'd started something unfathomable with a life all its own/ talking about being black n' back in a society that stifles our self expression/ unlocking doors we didn't even know had been closed/ I missed you/ I was thinking about you all the time/ about our conversations/ about being with you n' slow fingertips n' touching or being touched by you

***

Angelique

Lorena Gale

Lorena is an award-winning actress, director and writer. She has worked extensively in theatres across Canada, notably as May Buchanan in the Grand Theatre/Stage on Screen production of John Murrell's "Farther West", Normal Jean in "The Colored Museum", and Hecuba in "Age of Iron" at the Firehall Theatre, Vancouver for which she received a Jessie Richardson Award and nomination respectively. Her numerous film and television credits include *Broken Trust* with Tom Selleck, *Serving in Silence* with Glenn Close, "The X Files", and a leading role in the Lifestyle network program "Ebbie".

An emerging writer and solo performer, Lorena has recently published articles in *Canadian Theatre Review* and *CanPlay*, and her personal essay, "Where Beauty Sits" will be published in *But Where Are You Really From?* , an anthology. "Angelique", which marks Lorena's playwriting debut, is a winner of the duMaurier Arts Ltd. National Playwriting Competition.

Angelique

Lorena Gale

*Marie Josephe Angelique, a slave in 1734 who has been
accused of setting a fire which destroyed a large portion
of Montréal. In this passage she has recently given birth
to a child from an unwanted liaison with her master,
François de Francheville. Here, she talks to the child
before taking its life.*

ANGELIQUE alone with the baby.

ANGELIQUE

In the beginning there was darkness. Dense. Profound. Darkness. Like a
thick black blanket stretching into seamless infinity. The darkness was all
and all was darkness. Is and would ever be. And the darkness slumbered.
Complete in her ebony world.

'Til one day there was a movement. A stirring. A rumbling somewhere
deep inside. An unacknowledged longing to be more than everything.
Growing like the sound of distant thunder. Unsettling her dreams. But not
enough to wake her.

The stirring grew into a churning. The darkness swirled and eddied. Rising
and crashing in on herself. She rocked. She reeled. Until she woke. And
then she knew that she would never sleep again.

"Something has changed in me. I can no longer bear to be alone."

And with that thought the darkness heaved and pushed. Heaved and
pushed. Forcing desire from her depths. Giving birth to light.

Light was small. No bigger than a spark. But in it, darkness could see the
full extent of herself.

"I am so much more than what I thought I was."

And light blinked with the bright eyes of a newborn. Dazzling. Delighting the darkness. And a great heat she had never before noticed spread through darkness as she closed protectively 'round light. Like a mother cradling her child.

Light, unlike darkness, came into being complete with its own self-knowledge — which it fed on with a ferocious hunger. Growing fatter. And pushing back the darkness in defiance. The darkness, being everywhere, still encompassed the light no matter how she strained to give it room.

The light, fueled by its own existence, grew hotter in confinement.

"I am so much more than what I am. At least as much as darkness — which is everywhere. Why must I be contained? Without me, the darkness has no knowledge of itself. Therefore I am everything. And the darkness is nothing."

The light burned with greater arrogance. Growing hotter and denser with a simmering anger, which bubbled and popped beneath its surface of brilliance.

'I am more than...I am more than this...I am more than this,' it seethed.

'Til it was so full of itself that it exploded, sending shards of its being hurling through the darkness and lighting up the void.

The light was now everywhere. Cutting through the darkness with the sharpness of an ax. Cruelly severing the umbilicus between them. The darkness was so blinded by the light that she could no longer see. And so retreated to where she could have some sense of herself. Though light still pierced her — as a reminder that it now ruled everything.

Light and darkness.

That is how the two became separate forces. In constant opposition. Light in the forefront. And darkness. Waiting on the edge of everything.

When the first white man came to our village, he was no surprise to us. Because we had observed light and dark play itself out in everything around us. Even you, my baby. Where light and dark have clashed and come together. When we saw those white faces, we knew the explosion had come and the long period of waiting had begun. And so we walked towards our destiny. Our heads held high. Our eyes wide open.

But there is something else we know, my child. That in the end...the darkness reclaims everything. The stars will fall. The sun will cease to shine. Light will collapse in on itself. 'Til once again, it is nothing more than just a little spark. That flickers, sputters, pops itself out. The darkness will resume her peaceful reign.

But that day is a long way off. I will never see it. Neither will you, my baby. So light. So powerfully dark.

> *She puts her hand over the baby's face,*
> *suffocating it.*

Fly home and greet the darkness. There are others waiting there. Mama loves you and will join you soon.

***

Sixty Below

Leonard Linklater & Patti Flather

Leonard Linklater is a First Nations journalist and playwright. He was born and raised in Inuvik, North West Territories, and has lived in Whitehorse for 18 years. He is a member of the Vuntut Gwich'in First Nation and Director of Radio at Northern Native Broadcasting Yukon.

Patti Flather is an Anglo-Canadian of English, Scottish and Irish descent. She grew up in North Vancouver, British Columbia. She is a journalist, playwright, and fiction writer who has lived in the Yukon since 1988.

Sixty Below

Leonard Linklater & Patti Flather

December in the Yukon. Henry is finally out of jail!
This time he's going to stay out, lay off the booze and
make relationship with Rosie work. But Dave and Big
Joe don't like the change in their old drinking buddy.
And Winter Solstice is around the corner - which is
when Johnnie died one year ago, up the Long Lake
Road, on a night out with the boys. Ruth, his wife, is
determined to get some answers. Rosie is Johnnie's
sister.

Scene Nine. RUTH'S apartment. The women
are drinking cider and eating pizza. RUTH is
getting quite drunk.

ROSIE   B-15! Why couldn't it have been B-15!

RUTH   Shut up and have another cider.

ROSIE   I'm always one number off!

RUTH   Kiss another thirty bucks good-bye. Do you think
we'll ever win the jackpot?

ROSIE   One number! That's all I needed, fuckin' B-15!

RUTH   Eight thousand beautiful dollars! That would buy
us a night on the town!

ROSIE   You and me... we'd be crazy!

RUTH   We don't need a jackpot for that! We're crazy
                   anyway!

ROSIE   Like this summer. We were bad! Remember those
                   guys? What did they call you?

RUTH   (*acting sexy*) Hello, I'm Raunchy Ruth!

ROSIE   They really thought they were going to get lucky.
                   (*putting on a Texan accent, imitating the guys that
                   tried to pick them up*) "How's about another peach
                   cider, my little Yukon Rose?"

RUTH   We'll have two more peach ciders, please. And
                   don't forget the Tequila shooters. And bring extra
                   limes for my little sister here. And what about the
                   way you were slow dancing with that guy —
                   what's his face?

ROSIE   (*laughing at the name*) Arnold!

RUTH   Arnold and Mervyn!

ROSIE   From Alaska.

RUTH   God I'd never get it on with an army boy.

ROSIE   Yea. Little crewcuts...

BOTH   ...little hard-ons.

                   They crack up laughing together.

ROSIE   If Henry found out, he'd flip!

RUTH   My lips are sealed.

ROSIE   They better be! Or I'm up shit creek.

RUTH   I know how to keep a secret.

ROSIE	Speaking or secrets...I'm trying to decide how to tell Henry about the diploma. I want to do something special. How should I do it?
RUTH	Hmmmm...I know! Give him a blow job! He'll be so happy you can tell him anything!
ROSIE	(*laughing*) No! Something romantic.
RUTH	How much more romantic can you get for a guy then a blow job?!
ROSIE	I could make him a nice dinner. Steak and potatoes. With candles. And for dessert...cheesecake!
RUTH	He ain't worth all that trouble.
ROSIE	I have to do something nice. I feel like I cheated on him.
RUTH	That's not cheating.
ROSIE	I told Henry everything before this.
RUTH	You're not embarrassed, are you?
ROSIE	About what?
RUTH	About finishing top in your class. You know how guys are, they get weird about stuff like that. If you do anything better than them, they feel insecure or something.
ROSIE	You're so cynical. Henry wants to go back to school too.
RUTH	Henry?! No way!
ROSIE	That's what he told me. He did a lot of thinking in jail. He went to sweatlodges and everything.
RUTH	Oh that means a lot. Everyone knows that's where you go to smoke dope. They have a few tokes and use the sage and sweetgrass to hide the smell.

ROSIE   Really?

RUTH   It's common knowledge. You know, I'm so proud
             of you. I wish I had my grade twelve.

ROSIE   I thought you did.

RUTH   I was so close. Only two more courses, that's all I
             needed. I would have been the first in my family to
             graduate. Then I got pregnant. Johnnie wanted me
             to stay home with the baby.

ROSIE   Johnnie sure loved Tyler. His first boy.

RUTH   Yeah, I put my life on hold for that guy, and he
             was hardly ever around, except with the guys. And
             now I'm stuck with three kids, trying to make ends
             meet. Never enough money...Johnnie didn't leave
             me anything. Now, I don't have a life and I don't
             have Johnnie.

ROSIE   Do you ever think about seeing other guys?

RUTH   I would if I could get 'em into bed and kick 'em out
             before morning. But men hang around like puppy
             dogs waiting for their breakfast. Next thing you
             know, you're waiting on them hand and foot.

ROSIE   It might be good for the boys to have a father
             again.

RUTH   (*suddenly angry*) Johnnie was their father!

ROSIE   Sorry.

                    Uncomfortable silence.

RUTH   (*trying to lighten the mood*) Besides, when do I
             have time for guys? Work and kids and meetings
             and laundry...and I've got to leave time for the
             occasional girls night out, don't I?

ROSIE   I know it's been hard for you. It's not easy for me either. I dream about Johnnie all the time. Sometimes I even talk to him. In the morning I wake up crying.

Both women are fighting back tears.

RUTH   I miss him so much it hurts. Sometimes I see him and I try to touch him and there's nothing there. I'm reaching into the air, trying to grab hold of an answer. Other times I see them all down on Long Lake Road. They're doing something, but I don't know what. Then I hear gunshots and scream and wake up shaking. I keep waiting for a time that I can sleep through the night again. I don't want to miss him anymore.

ROSIE   We never nagged Johnnie, did we?

RUTH   What?

ROSIE   Got on his case. You know.

RUTH   Did Henry put that stupid idea into your head?

ROSIE   No. I was just thinking. I used to bug Johnnie to study music. He was so good at it.

RUTH   Nothing wrong with that. He was good at a lot of things.

Both women are crying now.

ROSIE   Maybe he took it the wrong way, like I didn't love him or something.

RUTH   I used to tell him he could do better. But it wasn't like I bugged him all the time. I just wanted the best for him.

ROSIE   I just wanted him to dream a little.

RUTH   Me too.

ROSIE   Ruth?

RUTH   Yeah?

ROSIE   What if...he thought we didn't love him?

> *They hug each other and cry on each other's shoulder.*

RUTH   Big finale to our night on the town.

ROSIE   Yeah.

> *Both women laugh to release tension.*

ROSIE   It might be easier if you had a man around. Easier for the kids too.

RUTH   Oh sure, rent a Dad. I'll go down to Hougen's and order one right now.

ROSIE   I don't mean like that. Isn't there anybody you're interested in?

RUTH   Look, I know you're real happy 'cause you got your man back. But if it weren't for those guys Johnnie would be sitting here with me now. It's their fault.

ROSIE   You don't really mean that.

RUTH   I do. I hate them for that night. Johnnie never would commit suicide. Maybe he fooled around on me. But there were things Johnnie would never do. He never drove if he was really drunk. How drunk does a guy have to be to kill himself? And why would he bring his friends along to watch?

ROSIE   What are you saying?

RUTH   Those guys know something they're not telling. What were they doing out at Long Lake, in the middle of the night, pissed to the gills — hunting?! Did one of them think Johnnie was a moose? Did one of them trip on a log and blow his head off? Maybe there was a fight? You know how Henry gets when he's drunk...he'll pick a fight with anybody.

ROSIE   Henry loved Johnnie! They all did. None of those guys would ever hurt Johnnie.

RUTH   They were all jealous of him.

ROSIE   You're crazy. You're not thinking straight. You've had too much to drink and you don't mean that.

RUTH   Yes I do. They killed Johnnie and they're gonna pay. And you better watch out or Henry will hurt you too.

ROSIE   You're wrong!

RUTH   You gotta stay away from Henry. Get rid of him.

ROSIE   No! I love him!

RUTH   There's a lot of stuff you don't know about Henry. You don't know how many times he's lied to you. How many times he's played around on you.

ROSIE   I don't believe you. Why are you saying these things?

RUTH   Because I know! Everyone thinks Johnnie was a saint! But when he came home, he was totally different. Half the time he didn't come home at all. Out screwing around...and Henry too! The two of them out fucking around...

ROSIE   No! Henry wouldn't do that to me!

RUTH   The sooner you get away from that guy the better

ROSIE   I can't listen to you! I gotta go!

ROSIE runs out.

*

Scene Ten. ROSIE returns to her apartment.
She is still upset about her fight with RUTH.
HENRY is mad about finding the diploma.
JOE is passed out on the couch.

ROSIE   Hi!

HENRY   (*smelling booze*) Hi. Smells like you've been having fun.

ROSIE   Is that against the law?

HENRY   No.

ROSIE   Ruth and I had a few ciders while we were playing radio bingo.

HENRY   Glad you had fun.

ROSIE   You're in a fine mood.

HENRY   Is that against the law?

ROSIE   Guess not.

HENRY   Just how much fun did you have?

ROSIE   What's your problem?

HENRY   You know I'm trying not to drink. Two days back and you can't even hold off on the party with Ruth.

ROSIE   It wasn't a party!

HENRY   I just get out and already my old lady is getting tanked. Thanks for the support.

ROSIE   Wait a minute! I'm not the one who put you in jail. You've got to take some responsibility for that.

HENRY   I am! But...it'd be nice if you'd spend some time with me.

ROSIE   What, you don't want me to go out? You expect me to put my life on hold for you, just because you screwed up!

HENRY   I guess I'm suppose to jump through all these hoops for everyone, while all my friends, and my old lady are getting pissed right under my nose.

ROSIE   I'm not the one who drinks so much I fight with every guy in sight, and gets sent back to jail for assault...again!

HENRY   I told you, I'm laying off the booze!

ROSIE   And what about the dope? Those sweatlodges you told me about...smoking drugs wasn't one of the attractions, was it?

HENRY   Who gave you that idea?

ROSIE   Well it's pretty common knowledge that the guys in jail like to get stoned before they go in the sweatlodge.

HENRY   So a few of the guys got high. Sure. I never did. I wanted to respect the ceremony...Fuck! You don't have a clue what it's like in Matsqui.

ROSIE   Seems like I don't have a clue about a lot of things. If you really want to know, it wasn't much of a party at Ruth's. She says you and Johnnie did more than dance with all the girls. Like all those nights you never came home and said you crashed at Dave's place.

HENRY   That bitch. She's lying!

ROSIE   Did you, Henry? Did you cheat on me?

HENRY   No!

ROSIE	You wouldn't hide something like that from me?
HENRY	I told you I didn't! I should be asking you about hiding stuff. (*showing her the diploma*) Just a little something I found tucked away in a cupboard.
ROSIE	I guess it's not a surprise anymore.
HENRY	I guess not.
ROSIE	I'm sorry. You know you haven't been home very long...
HENRY	Takes a real long time to say, "Guess what Henry, I got my grade twelve." Must be all of three seconds.
ROSIE	I tried to tell you when you got back...
HENRY	All those months in jail, you couldn't slip it in during a phone call, or write it down in a letter.
ROSIE	Ruth thought I should surprise you.
HENRY	Oh, so you let Ruth decide what you're going to tell me!
ROSIE	No!
HENRY	And what else have you girls been up to?
ROSIE	I've been going to school and working, that's what I've been up to. When are you going to get a job?
HENRY	I told you, I'm going out wood-cutting. It's almost for sure.
ROSIE	Good. 'Cause the rent's due next week and I want to take a writing course up at the college.
HENRY	Was that going to be my next surprise?
ROSIE	You make it sound like I'm in a conspiracy against you.

HENRY	That's how it feels, you and Ruth together.
ROSIE	It was hard working and going to school. I'm sick of doing it all by myself, trying to pay the rent every month, and my tuition...you gotta help me.
HENRY	(*sarcastic*) Oh help me, Henry, the rent's due and I have to pay my tuition, it's really important to me even though I didn't tell you about my diploma.
ROSIE	You asshole! I waited nine months for you!
HENRY	Why? So you could hide things from me?
ROSIE	I wasn't hiding anything!
HENRY	(*sarcastic*) Oh no, I wouldn't hide anything from you Henry. Especially not in a fucking Kraft Dinner cupboard. (*angry*) You don't want to tell me anything so you stuff your precious diploma way the fuck up in the Kraft dinner cupboard!
ROSIE	You are so immature! You say you want to have kids...you're not ready to have kids!
HENRY	Fuck you! (*putting his coat on*)
ROSIE	Where are you going?
HENRY	Out! (*storming out*)
ROSIE	Well, fuck you too!

*

	Scene Eleven. JOHNNIE moves toward HENRY, who can see him now. HENRY is terrified. As he speaks, JOHNNIE drums and dances a frightening dance. HENRY hears voices in his head.
HENRY	Johnnie! Don't hurt me! I...I'm scared Johnnie! Nobody understands. Do you, Johnnie? I hope you

	do. I did so much praying in that sweatlodge. I tried to do what they said and look inside myself.
JOHNNIE	And to the Creator, and the grandmother and grandfather spirits.
ROSIE	It was like I could never come clean.
BIG JOE	I need help!
RUTH	You never needed anyone before.
ROSIE	At least that's what you said.
BIG JOE	I can't do it alone.
DAVE	Why not?
RUTH	I don't know.
HENRY	I'm scared.
ROSIE	You can do whatever you want.
BIG JOE	No! I can't.
DAVE	Nobody understands.
HENRY	I feel like I'm in a river now. It's flowing so fast. The icy water is just pushing me along, pushing and pushing...ah, there's pieces of ice in it. They're cutting me, and bruising me. Ouch! The beaver...its tail...right in front of me. Beaver is strong and sleek. Its fur glistens. I must grab onto the tail. Slow down! Wait! My boots are dragging me down. It's getting colder. The ice is cutting into me! The skidoo is at the river's edge. I'll never make it. There's nobody around.
DAVE	No, Henry! You're not far from shore.
BIG JOE	You can yell for help, and claw your way through the ice.
ROSIE	You're a strong man.

RUTH | No! You're little and weak.

HENRY | Come on, you're a survivor, Henry.

BIG JOE | You're strong because you've come through a lot and you're still alive...

ROSIE | You know what I'm talking about.

> *HENRY hesitates as if grappling with a truth he doesn't like.*

HENRY | (*after a beat*) Why did they have to fight like that? Why did they have to drink and fight and hit each other? Why did they let us see that? Goddamn you! Goddamn you both! It wasn't fair.

JOHNNIE | No, it wasn't. People make mistakes.

RUTH | Yeah, they make mistakes. I know...

ROSIE | Some of our people have forgotten things that used to help them.

JOHNNIE | Like talking to the grandmother and grandfather spirits, and learning from the elders, and being proud of ourselves...

HENRY | How can I be proud of myself with boots stuck in the bottom of this goddamn river!

RUTH | Okay, Henry, die on that river bottom.

ROSIE | Say good-bye to Rosie.

BIG JOE | And your mother and father.

DAVE | And good-bye to yourself too.

HENRY | (*yelling*) Stop! Stop! Stop!

***

Index of playwrights

Index of plays

Beyond the Pale

Dramatic Writing from
First Nations Writers & Writers of Colour

Editors: Yvette Nolan • Betty Quan • George Seremba

Yvette Nolan is a playwright, director, performer and popular theatre facilitator born in Prince Albert, Saskatchewan to an Algonquin mother and an Irish immigrant father. She lives in Winnipeg where she has worked in virtually every capacity in theatre, from administrator to archivist to actor. She first emerged as a playwright with her critically and popularly acclaimed play, "Blade".

Betty Quan was born in Vancouver and now lives in Toronto where she works as a freelance editor and writer. Her work encompasses radio and stage adaptations, and script consultation and editing. She has just served a residency at the Canadian Film Centre, and is currently developing her own two-hour teleplay, as well as adapting Joy Kogawa's "Naomi's Road" for a Young People's Theatre school tour, and is working on a libretto for a new opera, "Iron Road" for Tapestry Music Theatre.

George Bwanika Seremba was born in Uganda and started writing and acting at Makerere University, but came into his own as an artist during his years o[...] in Kenya. Since moving to Canada he has appea[...] numerous plays across the country, feature film[...] television programs. Following the international [...] success of his play "Come Good Rain", he has re[...] completed his new play, "Napoleon of the Nile"[...]

ISBN 0-88754-542-4

61995

9 780887 545429